The New Examination System - GCSE

WALTER ROY

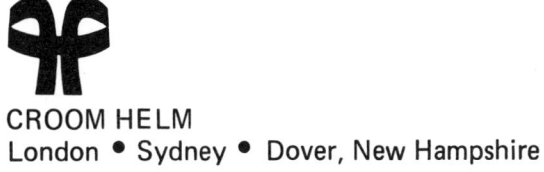

CROOM HELM
London • Sydney • Dover, New Hampshire

© 1986 Walter Roy
Croom Helm Ltd, Provident House, Burrell Row,
Beckenham, Kent BR3 1AT
Croom Helm Australia Pty Ltd, Suite 4, 6th Floor,
64-76 Kippax Street, Surry Hills, NSW 2010, Australia

British Library Cataloguing in Publication Data

Roy, Walter
    The new examination system: the General
    Certificate of Secondary Education, GCSE.
    1. General certificate of secondary
    education examination (Great Britain)
    I. Title
    373.12'62   LB3056.G7

ISBN 0-7099-4217-6

Croom Helm, 27 South Main Street,
Wolleboro, New Hampshire 03894-2069

Library of Congress Cataloging-in-Publication Data

Roy, Walter.
    The new examination system.

    Includes index.
    1. General Certificate of Secondary Education.
I. Title.
LB3056.G7R69   1986   373.12'6   86-11666
ISBN 0-7099-4217-6

Printed and bound in Great Britain
by Billing & Sons Limited, Worcester.

CONTENTS

		Page
PREFACE		
1.	Introduction: Past, Present and Future	1
2.	Subjects and Syllabuses: The National Criteria	19
3.	Assessment and Certification	42
4.	G.C.S.E.: - Inside the School	65
5.	The New Examining Groups	80
6.	G.C.S.E. - Through Students' Eyes	106
7.	A Plan for Action	134
APPENDIX:	GCSE Examining Groups in England and Wales	164
Index		167

PREFACE

THE NEW EXAMINATION SYSTEM: THE GENERAL CERTIFICATE
                              OF SECONDARY EDUCATION
                              (GCSE)

The reform of the public examination system for sixteen year old students present a considerable challenge to secondary schools. The new General Certificate of Secondary Education, to be available from 1988, but being implemented from 1986, is more than a continuation and a combination of the present General Certificate of Education (GCE) 'O' level and the Certificate of Secondary Education (CSE) examinations. New syllabuses, new systems of assessing and grading pupils' achievements are subject to national ground rules - the national criteria - evolved by the Secretary of State for Education and Science, and supervised by the Secondary Examinations Council. New examining bodies are emerging and schools accustomed to exercising considerable autonomy in designing their curricula are having to come to terms with constraints imposed not only by external pressures, but by a severe resource crisis brought about by the cuts in educational expenditure.

How can schools cope with this challenge? How far will the new examination system reflect what is actually taught in our classrooms? What are its new features? Which pupils will be entered and with what prospects of success? How will the users of the examination system - the worlds of work and of higher education - respond to the changes? Above all, how will pupils, teachers and parents react? How can schools meet the tight time schedule, which requires work to start on new syllabuses by the autumn of 1986, with candidates being ready to enter for the first examinations in 1988, unless there is a postponement?

The book tries to answer some of these questions, and to provide an up-to-date picture of the examination world, with indications of future developments in the vital years ahead. The first two chapters examine the relationship between the existing G.C.E. 'O' level and C.S.E. examinations and the new G.C.S.E., with a detailed examination of the new syllabuses to be taught, and the national ground rules which have emerged. The third chapter deals with the new methods of assessment and certification, and considers the impact of the new grading system on schools and the introduction of criteria referencing, a new technique in the whole business of examinations. Chapters four and six look at G.C.S.E. from within, one providing a model for schools to cope with the changes and the other giving accounts of what the pupils themselves think of examinations, perhaps a novel, but necessary dimension in considering changes in education. Chapter five considers the constitutional and administrative changes in the structure of examination boards; chapter seven sees the need to relate the changes taking place inside schools to the outside world, and provides a plan for action to get the new system off the ground in a purposeful and effective manner.

Whatever the limitations of our public examinations, they are likely to remain firmly rooted in an educational system where change is effected by gradual rather than radical methods. Existing certificates, both at G.C.E. 'O' level and C.S.E. level, have a reputation for integrity, for providing incentives for students and teachers, and, on the whole, are generally accepted by employers and the world of higher education. The challenge for the new G.C.S.E. is to maintain the integrity of the system, whilst projecting its purpose, and methodology, into a new decade.

The book aims to assist those immediately and urgently concerned with implementing a far reaching educational reform; teachers and heads in schools, educational administrators in local authorities, and examiners and staff of the examination boards, with whom the author is in daily contact, have expressed the need for up-to-date information. But the students who are to be examined, their parents, school governors, higher education selectors, employers and the interested public, will all want to know what G.C.S.E., is about. The book should go some way towards meeting such needs.

The author is grateful for the tremendous help received from colleagues in the teaching profession, to members and staffs of examination boards, particularly those of the East Anglian

PREFACE

Regional C.S.E. Board, the London Regional C.S.E. Board, and the University of London Schools Examinations Board, and to many others concerned with examinations. Special thanks are due to the students of the Hewett School, Norwich, who provided the material for chapter six, to my indefatigable Secretary, Nancy, who typed the manuscript, Miss Mary Thompson, Secretary of the East Anglian Board for her comments, and to my wife, not only for reading, but encouraging me to write the book.

Walter Roy.

Chapter One

INTRODUCTION: PAST, PRESENT AND FUTURE

When the General Certificate of Education was first introduced in 1951 it broke new ground. The notion of a single subject examination, as distinct from the old school certificate which required candidates to pass in a group of subjects, reflected the widely held belief that individual children possessed different aptitudes, and that the curriculum in schools should both recognise, and provide for, such differences. The 1944 Education Act, still relatively new on the statute book, emphasised the right of each child to be educated according to "age, ability and aptitude". But the aspirations behind the Act represented a striving towards equality of opportunity, an opening of doors towards goals previously closed to all but a few. What mattered was the individual child; it was the business of the schools to shape a curriculum which suited the child, and the business of public examinations to reflect that curriculum rather than lead it. The schools were the masters and the examination boards the servants. Even before the introduction of comprehensive schools, the notions that a larger number of subjects should be taught in the new secondary schools, that there should be an element of choice for the majority of pupils, providing a balanced curriculum, had taken firm root. As yet, in the early 'fifties, the debate about examinations reform centred largely around the twenty per cent deemed capable of achieving G.C. 'O' levels in five or more subjects - those selected for grammar schools - to ensure for them a passport to higher education. But the single subject examination was intended to reflect individual differences give scope for individual talents, and allow for a differentiated curriculum, rather than the group or core mentality underlying the old school certificate.

INTRODUCTION: PAST, PRESENT AND FUTURE

The new secondary modern schools, which formed part of the tripartite system of grammar, technical and modern schools, created by the 1944 Education Act, were to be free from the shackles of external examinations altogether.

The G.C.E. certainly got off the ground as a successful single subject examination. No one of any standing within the educational fraternity seemed to quarrel with the fact that the universities continued to have the major say in what the schools should examine, with the examination boards based on Oxford and Cambridge leading the field at least in the public eye, but London University, and the Joint Matriculation Board in the North, being senior partners in a firmly entrenched examination establishment. The newly founded Associated Examining Board broke new ground in offering G.C.E. 'O' and 'A' level subjects not only in the conventional subjects taught in schools, but also examining subjects with a vocational flavour, such as engineering, technical drawing, and commerce usually taught in further education colleges. These reflected the growing points in the curriculum and the conviction that subjects with a vocational slant had a definite place in the G.C.E. system. The Associated Examining Board was not directly associated with, nor controlled by any university, and was immediately popular with technical schools and further education establishments, subsequently gaining considerable ground in schools which liked its 'new look' G.C.E. syllabuses.

But the most remarkable feature of the new G.C.E. 'O' level examination was its success with employers. The idea that it was to be a preparation for the limited number of students proceeding to higher education, mainly via the 'A' level route, was quickly abandoned in favour of the G.C.E. being considered a passport to good jobs. One employer after another and a multiplicity of public and private institutions demanded, and accepted, G.C.E. 'O' level passes, usually in five subjects, always including English and mathematics, as the hallmark of a successfully completed secondary education at sixteen. The new secondary modern schools were not slow to get the message. The notion of equality of opportunity, albeit as yet through differentiated schooling involving selection at 11+, was not seen through the abandonment of examinations, but rather by giving secondary modern youngsters a chance to take the G.C.E. This movement gained considerable ground in the early and mid 'fifties, when one

INTRODUCTION: PAST, PRESENT AND FUTURE

secondary modern school after another introduced G.C.E. 'O' level for its brighter pupils, achieving results which were often markedly better than those attained by the bottom third of grammar school pupils who had, five years earlier, succeeded in passing the 11-plus examination. Such success by pupils rejected at an early age as not being suitable for an academic education, demonstrated to the world at large the inaccuracy of 11-plus and certainly helped to prepare the way for the establishment of comprehensive schools. There were of course, various social, political and economic factors which also furthered the comprehensive school movement. By the late 'fifties, G.C.E. 'O' level was firmly established in the secondary modern schools of the country.

But the success of the secondary modern school in giving a minority of their pupils a chance to gain usually respectable, often good, and sometimes outstanding, examination results, exacted its price. What about the rest of the pupils in those schools who had no access to G.C.E. and indeed, to no public examinations at all? What was wrong with giving them an examination which they could pass, even if G.C.E. 'O' level was too academic and unsuitable? As pressure built up for more and more candidates to take the G.C.E. in those schools, so the unsuitability of an examination designed for the top twenty per cent became painfully obvious. More and more pupils were entered, often with little chance of success. Far from wanting to be free from the shackles of external examinations, the schools themselves, reflecting the aspirations of pupils and parents, and the desires of teachers, wanted both the incentive within and the passport without. This led to the establishment of a large number of different examinations available for school pupils. The Chamber of Commerce and City & Guilds certificates, other certificates awarded by the Union of Educational Institutions, met the need for those who had an emergent vocational aim, but not for others. There emerged a vast number of local certificates all over the country, designed and administered by teachers in their own schools, with the support of local education authorities. These were usually designed by groups of local schools, and bore the title of the locality, e.g. 'The Luton Proficiency Certificate'. These developments demonstrated the need for the availability of an examination, which was nationally recognised but easier to pass than the difficult

INTRODUCTION: PAST, PRESENT AND FUTURE

G.C.E. '0' levels. It thus prepared the way for the emergence of the Certificate of Secondary Education Examination (C.S.E) following the report of the Beloe 1 Committee, set up to consider the whole issue in the early 'sixties.

The report of the Beloe Committee was accepted by the Government in 1962, and was hailed as a piece of major educational reform; the schools responded enthusiastically to the idea that C.S.E. should co-exist with G.C.E.'0' level for sixteen year olds, and that school teachers rather than university dons should shape the new examination. Some of the features of the G.C.E. were inevitably reproduced in C.S.E.: the secondary school curriculum was subject orientated, and it followed that the new examination had to be a single subject examination. Similarly, the idea that an examination could only be passed by some pupils was still well entrenched, so that a target group had to be identified. This target group was seen as the forty per cent below the twenty per cent being currently prepared for the G.C.E. '0' level examination, so that some sixty per cent of the school population now had access to nationally recognised certification. But C.S.E., pioneered a number of new features which are clearly reflected in the new General Certificate of Secondary Education (GCSE) to be available from 1988. First, there was the abandonment of the pass/fail concept, a radical break with G.C.E., whereby some passed, and others, many others, failed each year. The new C.S.E. grading system, whereby pupils were awarded grades 1,2,3, 4 or 5, below which an ungraded performance was still recorded on the result slip, already contained the seeds of the idea developed by Sir Keith Joseph, that pupils should show what they could do rather than being penalised for what they could not. Continuous assessment of work done over the last two years of secondary schooling, and a substantial element of oral examining, not only in English and modern languages, but in other subjects, often including mathematics and history, at the option of teachers, were distinctly new features, reflecting new and more adventurous teaching styles particularly in the new comprehensive schools, forming a sharp contrast with the largely written approach to assessment followed in the grammar schools. The growing points in the curriculum were clearly reflected in the range of subjects available, which grew at a fast, and for some users, an alarming rate.

Three difference modes of examining were

INTRODUCTION: PAST, PRESENT AND FUTURE

established by the C.S.E. Boards: Mode 1 examinations were based on syllabuses designed by subject panels, consisting very largely of the teachers in the regions served by a C.S.E. board and were purely external examinations, papers being marked by the boards' examiners. Mode 2 syllabuses were based on agreements by groups of schools in a particular area, but still wishing to have external examinations for their candidates. Finally, mode 3 were entirely school based syllabuses, designed and examined by teachers in an individual school, though subject to external moderation. The development of mode 3 was a radical break with the established tradition of examining. Diversity was seen as a virtue, and it was expected from the examination boards to provide the appropriate service. Two C.S.E. boards in particular, the East Anglian and the West Yorkshire and Lindsey Boards, positively encouraged mode 3, and the number of such syllabuses designed by individual schools soon reached a thousand, with careful external moderation monitoring internal marking and assessment.

The C.S.E., following the Beloe recommendation, was founded on the philosophy of teacher control. In the heyday of the 'sixties, the teachers were the pioneers: they knew what they were doing, what was required, and it was not only logical but right, that they should decide the syllabuses, set the standards and run the examination boards. The constitutions of the C.S.E. boards therefore had an inbuilt teacher majority; the profession was in charge of its own destiny, at least as far as the new examination was concerned. But a number of problems soon reared their heads: first, there was the question of those borderline pupils who might just succeed in getting a G.C.E. 'O' level, or who might just fail that examination; should they be entered for G.C.E., or C.S.E., or both examinations? Parental pressure continued to run firmly in favour of the well-established G.C.E., with entries for that examination extending well beyond the supposed twenty-five per cent target group. An attempt to solve the dilemma was made by establishing the equivalence of C.S.E. Grade 1 with 'O' level grades, A, B and C. After initial skirmishes, a C.S.E. Grade 1 was accepted throughout the world of education and employment as equivalent to a pass at 'O' level, and it appeared that a solution had been found. Further flexibility appeared to be encouraged when the G.C.E. boards followed their C.S.E. partners and abolished the pass/fail concept,

INTRODUCTION: PAST, PRESENT AND FUTURE

declaring all their grades, now designated by the letters, A,B,C,D,E, to be passes, although most people realised that a pass really meant getting one of the first three grades.

But further problems remained. What was to be done with all those pupils who were outside the Beloe definition of C.S.E., i.e. the remaining forty per cent deemed not to be capable of passing any examination, referred in the Newsom report^2 as 'the other half?' However, it became quickly evident that these forty per cent were not to be done out of their chance of having a try in C.S.E., particularly in the vital subjects of English and mathematics. Again, a pragmatic solution was found: the C.S.E. boards accepted the notion of 'limited grade' syllabuses, whose content was lighter, less complex and therefore, within the reach of the less able youngsters. Such syllabuses were limited in the sense that candidates being entered would usually obtain a grade no higher than a 3, a procedure which the new G.C.S.E. examination will adopt in setting certain questions aimed at candidates from the lower ability ranges. Thus, C.S.E., particularly in English and maths, but also in a host of other subjects, became available for more and more candidates, reaching the eightieth percentile ranks. The idea of a forty per cent target group for C.S.E. below the twenty per cent deemed capable of passing 'O' level was soon abandoned. Whatever criticisms made of the straight jacket of external examinations, whatever the problems of convincing parents, employers and the youngsters themselves that C.S.E. was worth having, even below Grade 1, the demand for the examination soon extended almost throughout the ability range, with schools often entering whole year groups except remedial pupils. C.S.E. might not have the academic respectability of the well-established 'O' level, but it compensated by giving a chance to many more girls and boys to show what they could do, by its introduction of syllabuses which were often closely related to the pupils' everyday lives and experiences, and by developing examination techniques based on the extensive use of oral examining and continuous assessment, thereby reducing the dependence on formal written papers with rigid time limits.

In the meantime, the schools were having to come to terms with the existence of a dual system of examination at 16+, which, as it developed, showed up not only considerable strains and stresses in

INTRODUCTION: PAST, PRESENT AND FUTURE

school organisation, but was also seen as socially divisive particularly by the more fervent advocates of comprehensive schools. What was the point, they said, of abandoning the 11+ examinations and having a unified secondary system if the examination system itself continued to be divisive? How could teachers make really accurate judgments as to whether the G.C.E. or the C.S.E. was the most suitable target at 14, when such notions had been rejected at 11? Since teaching groups aiming at one or the other examination, had to be identified at the beginning of the 4th year, the sorting out of G.C.E. and C.S.E. candidates had to take place during the third year; in the larger comprehensive schools, this meant that sorting processes began in the spring term of that year, earlier than many teachers, pupils and parents thought wise or appropriate.

Alongside the establishment of the dual system of examinations, a number of other developments took place in the comprehensive schools which already pointed the way towards the need for a common examination system; first, there was the emergence of mixed ability teaching, standard practice in many comprehensive schools in the early years, following what was happening in the primary schools. More frequently, mixed ability groups co-existed with setting arrangements. Whilst English, mathematics, foreign languages, and traditional sciences-physics, chemistry and biology - continued to be setted, often in G.C.E. or C.S.E. sets, the emergence of the option system, whereby pupils, in consultation with teachers and parents, chose four, five or six subjects at the beginning of the 4th year, created teaching groups containing a wide ability range of pupils, even when this was not intended by the school administration. The idea of grouping pupils according to interest rather than ability gained considerable ground. If the school required Jill or John to include at least one science and at least one humanities subject, those who selected human biology and geography in preference to chemistry and history, often found themselves in mixed ability 'option' groups, aiming either at G.C.E. or C.S.E., or both.

But for teachers, pupils and parents the strains and stresses of the dual system were seen most clearly during the 3rd year, i.e. at 14, when decisions had to be made as to whether a particular pupil should follow a G.C.E. or C.S.E. course. Parental pressure was clearly towards the well established G.C.E. examination; whatever the

INTRODUCTION: PAST, PRESENT AND FUTURE

advantages of the C.S.E., however good its presentation by the school, the need for making such a decision at all, led to unhappiness and sometimes disagreement between the various parties, and certainly between many parents and teachers, with the pupil caught in the middle. Schools felt themselves responsible for ensuring that candidates were successful and for those well outside the G.C.E. target group, success meant entering them for the C.S.E. Parents, on the other hand, often felt that since the G.C.E. existed and could be taken, their children should have a chance to present themselves for it, whatever the teachers' views.

Schools have attempted to deal with this situation in various ways: dual entries for both G.C.E. and C.S.E. in the same subject became widespread in certain subjects, whose syllabuses do not diverge greatly. Many schools with sixth forms encourage the 'topping up' of C.S.E's with an 'O' level, certainly in the first year sixth. The overloading of candidates with a multiplicity of papers, the cost of dual entries to two different boards, the burden of complex administrative work, clearly indicate some of the problems of the dual system. The emergence of the job of 'examinations officer', a post of responsibility in most secondary schools held by a teacher, reflects the need to cope with a growing work load, diverting energy and attention from teaching.

Even more serious however, have been the difficulties experienced by the smaller secondary schools, an increasing number as school rolls fall. Such schools may not be able to timetable separate G.C.E. and C.S.E. groups at all, or only at the cost of moving resources away from younger age groups. As staffing cuts and reduction in staffing establishments have become the order of the day in nearly all local education authorities, increasing numbers of previously separate teaching groups have had to go by the board; indeed, there is growing evidence that some subjects, previously available both at C.S.E. and G.C.E. 'O' level, are available for one examination only, or at worst, not at all. This means that many secondary pupils no longer have access to a balanced curriculum, with appropriate examination objectives. Falling rolls, tighter staffing establishments and over-stretched resources thus compounded the problems posed by the dual examination system.

It is not therefore surprising that movements

INTRODUCTION: PAST, PRESENT AND FUTURE

geared towards establishing a common system of examining at 16+ gained ground long before the present Secretary of State made the decision to introduce it. The pressure for such a system originated in the schools, where the problems of duality are felt most keenly. The Cambridge University Local Examinations Syndicate joined forces with the East Anglian C.S.E. Examinations Board to form the first consortium to offer 16+ examination in five subjects - mathematics, geography, English, technical drawing and biology. Joint subject panels were set up who were answerable to a steering committee composed of senior personnel from both sets of boards, and were required to produce examination papers suitable for approximately sixty per cent of the ability range. Some of these were common papers, others were already differentiated, additional papers or more difficult questions being geared towards the abler candidates, as will be the case with G.C.S.E. The candidates are entered for one examination only, the 16+, but obtain two certificates - a G.C.E. and a C.S.E. certificate. It is thus possible to gain both G.C.E. grades, ranging from A to E and C.S.E. grades, varying from 1 to 5, with ungraded performances also recorded. The system is known as 'two for the price of one'.

During the middle and late 'seventies, pressure on the government to establish a common system was building up rapidly. The Schools Council, the teachers' unions and the C.S.E. examination boards themselves, provided the impetus for such a movement, and certainly responded to it. Whilst there was some divergence of view between G.C.E. and C.S.E. boards, their community of interest appeared greater than any differences and the then Secretary of State, Shirley Williams, decided on a thorough appraisal of the problem. Waddell, a distinguished retired Civil Servant, was invited to chair a high powered committee of educationists, whose terms of reference was to look at the possibility of introducing a common system of examining. The main recommendations of the Waddell Committee were in favour of a common system. They included statements advising national criteria, school based and board based examinations, co-ordination of 16+ examinations by a central$_4$body, and a new structure of examination boards.

However, the Secretary of State still hesitated and with the establishment of a Conservative government in 1979, the whole issue

INTRODUCTION: PAST, PRESENT AND FUTURE

seemed to be shelved, at least for the time being. Although the new Conservative government seemed firmly wedded to the retention of G.C.E. '0' level, certainly whilst Mark Carlisle was Secretary of State, the movement in the schools towards a common system accelerated. More and more joint 16+ schemes got off the ground in nearly all parts of the country. The number of entries increased rapidly and most comprehensive schools, by 1980, were running one, two or more 16+ schemes. The Schools Council, a widely representative body of teachers, local authority officers and politicians, parents, employers, Her Majesty's Inspectors, in fact, education's parliament, and responsible for overseeing the public examination system, went on record in favour of a common system at 16+. Soon after Sir Keith Joseph was appointed Secretary of State for Education, he dissolved the Schools Council and in its place established the Secondary Examinations Council under the chairmanship of Sir Wilfred Cockcroft. This body was appreciably smaller than its predecessor and consisted of nominees directly appointed by the Secretary of State. Its brief was not only to oversee and develop the examination system in the country, but to report directly to the Secretary of State from whom it derived its authority and much of its money. But what sort of a system was it to develop? How long could the division between G.C.E. and C.S.E. be perpetuated, bearing in mind what was happening in the schools? As soon as the new Secondary Examinations Council had come to grips with the problem it recommended[5] exactly what its predecessor, the Schools Council had advocated: the need was for a common system.

For sometime, the Secretary of State was reluctant to accept that recommendation and talked about 'harmonising' the dual system rather than changing it. There was no doubt that among Conservative Members of Parliament, there was considerable pressure to retain the G.C.E. '0' level, that symbol of academic respectability still seen as a guarantee of standards and selectivity even within the comprehensive system. However, in spite of certain political pressures, the popular appeal of the common system was unmistakable, and finally, in June 1984, the Secretary of State announced the introduction of a common system to start in 1986, with the first G.C.S.E. examinations to be held in 1988. But it was evident, even before this decision was announced, that the freedom to which schools and examination boards had been accustomed, was to be

INTRODUCTION: PAST, PRESENT AND FUTURE

severely curtailed. First and foremost, the Secretary of State made it clear that each syllabus had to conform to national criteria, and that he himself had to be satisfied that such criteria was known to and followed by the designers of syllabuses. The following chapter looks in detail at the national criteria debate, the impact of the requirement on what is taught in school and examined by the boards. A new ad hoc body, a national council composed of representatives of both G.C.E. and C.S.E. boards was set up specifically to deal with the issue of national criteria, each syllabus being considered in the light of the new ground rules prescribed by the Secretary of State. This body brought together the experts from the examination world in the country, with G.C.E. and C.S.E. personnel sharing the task of drafting, amending and finally agreeing the national criteria for each subject. Many teachers and other educationists saw the exercise as an attempt by central government to gain control of the curriculum; others felt that even with the constraints imposed by national criteria, a common system was preferable to the duality with which schools had lived for some twenty years and the price was worth paying. By April 1985, the majority of syllabuses covering nearly all subjects taught in schools had been prepared, and firm guidelines relating to national criteria had either been worked out, or the Secretary of State's preferences accepted. Conformity to national policy had replaced the freedom to initiate which was so widely accepted twenty years earlier.

Apart from the concept of national criteria, the new examination, to be known as the General Certificate of Secondary Education, differs in a number of important aspects from both the G.C.E. and C.S.E.: first, the target group is to be almost the whole of the school population. The Secretary of State has stated that he expects between eighty and ninety per cent of the school population to be examined, thus going well beyond the Beloe notion of a target group of sixty per cent of examinable candidates. This extension of public examinations is to be accomplished by developing a system of assessment radically different from what is in operation at present: norm referencing, whereby marks are allocated to the questions on examination papers, with cut off points for grades often decided in advance of the marking, is to be replaced by criteria referencing, an entirely new approach.

INTRODUCTION: PAST, PRESENT AND FUTURE

Instead of testing candidates on what they might or might not know, the new examination is to concentrate on enabling them to show only what they do know. This complex and complicated exercise will be considered further in chapter 3, and has so far proved too difficult to be implemented quickly. It is already clear that the G.C.S.E. examination will start without the criteria referencing exercise being complete, and will therefore have to continue to use the present system of results being determined largely by norms.

Yet another feature of the new system is its grading system, featuring seven grades; A, B, C, D, E, F, G with ungraded performances also reported. A comparison between the present grading system and the new one shows the following differences:-

G.C.E. 'O' level	G.C.S.E.	C.S.E.
A	A)	
B	B)	1
C	C)	
D	D	2
E	E	3
UG	F	4
	G	5
	UG	UG

UG = ungraded performance

The intention, as announced by the Secretary of State is that average candidates, who are now deemed to be capable of achieving a Grade 4 C.S.E., should in the new examination, achieve at least a Grade F. This, the Secretary of State sees as an exercise in raising present standards. Furthermore, the most able candidates are to be given the opportunity of achieving a distinction certificate, and those immediately below the brightest a merit certificate although both proposals are still under discussion and meeting with considerable resistance.

The new examination is to be administered by five examining groups composed both of the G.C.E. and C.S.E. boards. The G.C.E. boards are given specific responsibility for monitoring the standards applicable to grades A, B and C, whereas the C.S.E. boards carry responsibility for the remaining grades of D,E,F,G and the ungraded performances. Thus, the separatism which is part of the dual system is perpetuated in the common system, although it is not yet clear just how these separate responsibilities will be carried out by the respective sets of boards, bearing in mind that the drafting of syllabuses, of examination papers, allocation of marks, assessment

INTRODUCTION: PAST, PRESENT AND FUTURE

procedures and moderating techniques are all being developed by joint subject panels drawn from both the G.C.E. and C.S.E. sectors.

All five examining groups, i.e. the London, Midland, Northern, Southern and Welsh groups, [6] have produced syllabuses in a wide range of subjects. Many of these were of course, already available as 16+ syllabuses, prior to the announcement that there was to be a common system. Others are entirely new, but nearly all examining groups have made a point of sending the draft syllabuses into schools for comment by school staffs before finalising the drafts. This is in itself, an unusual exercise, but has certainly crystallised teacher opinion as to approach, content and indeed the quality, of the new syllabuses. Unlike the C.S.E. examination, which is administered on a regional basis with schools having to enter candidates in their own regions, (unless exceptional arrangements are approved) G.C.S.E., will be available on a national basis and schools will be able to choose for which group of boards they wish their candidates to enter. This freedom of choice carries forward the principles of a free market in examination entries - and fees - a strong feature of the G.C.E. system. The timetable for the new examination is tight: the first examination is to be held in 1988, which means that those who reach the 4th year of secondary education in 1986, must start on the new syllabuses by the autumn of that year. As it has become clear that an enormous amount of developmental work still remains to be done, voices have increasingly been raised in favour of delaying the introduction of G.C.S.E.; the Association of County Councils (ACC) recently made representations to Sir Keith Joseph asking that the whole scheme should be delayed for at least another year, and submitting evidence showing that at least three times the resources being provided by the Secretary of State for training programmes alone, need to be available. Several teachers' unions, notably the NUT, have also come out in favour of delay, and it is possible that the recent industrial action by the teachers, which includes sanctions against participating in G.C.S.E. developmental work, being applied by the NUT and the NAS/UWT, may still force a delay, although the Secretary of State has stated firmly that he wishes to adhere to the proposed timetable. However, the examining groups, and many schools, are more interested in obtaining additional time for training staff, and certainly additional money for re-tooling

INTRODUCTION: PAST, PRESENT AND FUTURE

than in political controversy. Many teachers feel that now the decision has been taken, the sooner the schools are able to get on with a common system the better; others genuinely fear that an untidy and inadequate start will be made unless more time, and more money, are made available.

However, whatever the precise date of the start, the schools are having to plan for the implementation of a major reform of the public examination system within a remarkably short time: this involves thorough knowledge of the new syllabuses, decision by heads and school staffs in deciding which syllabuses to adopt, an understanding of the meaning of national criteria and its effect on teaching, developing the new grading system and switching to often new methods of assessment. But what is even more important and immediate, is the re-tooling required for the exercise. It is quite clear that decisions regarding choice of syllabuses will be heavily influenced by the resources available: there is not the money to buy vast numbers of new textbooks or equipment. Re-tooling will have to be a gradual process and those examining groups which have been particularly sensitive to this particular aspect of the exercise are likely to attract many customers.

Apart from the immense task of launching the G.C.S.E. examination in time for the new fourth years in 1986, schools will need to mount major publicity and public relations exercises to ensure that parents in particular, but also other interest groups, notably employers, understand the new system. How such a task may be tackled is considered in chapter 7.

The major problems relate both to the need for training and the difficulty of finding time to discuss new approaches and methods of implementing the policy change. Whilst many teachers have considerable experience of continuous assessment and oral examining where such features form part of the present system, others work in subject areas where written examination papers, confined to a few hours, is the only method of assessing the outcome of several years' secondary schooling. The insistence that continuous assessment should form part of every syllabus, the widespread use of oral work, the coming together of two different philosophies of examining require training programmes involving the whole secondary teaching force, all these have to be seen as a continuous process. This appears not to have been foreseen by

INTRODUCTION: PAST, PRESENT AND FUTURE

the Secretary of State, who has so far responded only with small sums for training which barely allow departmental heads to come to grips with the new situation. The need for the whole staff of each school to discuss, confer, plan and decide on the best method of implementing the change in the light of local circumstances is very real. The turbulence of the latest round of pay negotiations, the real pressures which exist in every school every day do not allow any spare time to do what needs to be done. At the very least, all schools need, before autumn 1986, a clear week, without the pupils coming in, to deal with the most pressing matters. The sooner this is recognised both by the government and the local education authorities, the better for all concerned.

Alongside the establishment of the new public examination system, other developments of considerable significance are taking place. In most schools it is increasingly recognised that examinations, however well designed, carefully monitored and respectably certificated, cannot portray the totality of achievements, the personalities and characteristics of young people. There is growing up in the secondary schools of the country, a powerful movement towards the introduction of profiles and records of achievements which are quite distinct from the development of the examination system, but no less demanding. Furthermore, the emergence of new curricular patterns, actively supported by the government, especially the technical and vocational educational initiative (TVEI) with a very different approach to syllabuses and assessments, make yet another set of demands. Finally, there is the emergence of the graded test movement, already well developed in the assessment of modern languages, but spreading rapidly to other subject areas, which point to yet another path which may be followed. The relationship between such developments and the introduction of the G.C.S.E., will need to be considered by each school in some detail. In some cases, the paths will clearly diverge; in others, there will be an integration of such features within the new system. Although there are interests which speak of the replacement of conventional examinations by profiles or records of achievement, there is within the foreseeable future, no likelihood that this will happen. The history of public examinations from the old school certificate in the 1930's, followed in the post war era by the

INTRODUCTION: PAST, PRESENT AND FUTURE

strongly developed G.C.E. 'O' and 'A' level system since the 'fifties, and the widespread use of C.S.E. in the 'sixties and 'seventies, point the same way: Schools want external examinations, whilst at the same time wanting to have a considerable say in how they are run and who runs them. There is no strong and vocal movement in favour of abolishing exams; the wishes of schools reflect and interpret the aspirations of a society, which expects examination boards, however constituted, to maintain recognised standards of achievement in given subjects at a certain age. The boards are seen both as controlling these standards and as acting with integrity and impartiality. It is therefore both necessary and prudent to plan the effective implementation of the new system.

Chapter One

REFERENCES

(1) <u>Secondary Schools Examinations other than G.C.E</u> Report of a Committee Appointed by Secondary Schools Examinations Council (Beloe Report). Ministry of Education, HMSO 1960.
(2) <u>Half our Future</u> - Report of the Central Advisory Council for Education (England) Newsom Report HMSO 1963.
(3) 'Setting' is streaming by subject, pupils being arranged in groups according to their ability in a subject.
(4) <u>School Examinations - Report of the Steering Committee to consider proposals for replacing the General Certificate of Education Ordinary level and the Certificate of Secondary Education examinations by a common system of examining - Waddell Report.</u> HMSO 1978.
(5) <u>Arguments for a common system of examining at 16+.</u> Schools Council 1973.
<u>A common system of examining at 16+</u> Evans/Methuen, 1971 - Schools Council Examinations Bulletin No. 23.
Review of comments on examinations bulletin 23 '<u>a common system of examining at 16+</u>'. Schools Council 1973. (Pamphlet : 12).
<u>Schemes of assessment</u>: experimental examinations for a common system of examining at 16+. Schools Council 1974 - (Pamphlet : 15)
<u>Examinations at 16+ proposals for the future.</u> Schools Council 1975.
<u>National co-ordination for a single system of examining at 16+.</u> Schools Council 1980.
<u>Determining standards in the proposed single system of examining at 16+</u>, by Lee Orr and Desmond Nuttall. Schools Council 1983. (Comparability in examinations occasional paper : 2).

REFERENCES

(6) <u>The Northern Ireland Schools Examinations Board</u> is similarly involved, but has not been included as this study deals specifically with the school system of England and Wales. The Northern Ireland Board is however an active partner in G.C.S.E., and hosted the Standing Conference of C.S.E. boards in October 1985.

Chapter Two

SUBJECTS AND SYLLABUSES: THE NATIONAL CRITERIA

The syllabus is the teacher's major operational tool. It determines to a very large extent, not only what is taught, but the methodology of teaching and the outcome of the teaching process. It is, at one and the same time, a major source of educational advancement and a place from which teachers and pupils are forever seeking to escape. The greatest criticism levelled against the G.C.E. examination, sometimes unfairly, has related to the restrictive nature of the syllabuses of G.C.E. boards. The majority of these boards are tied by history and constitution to the universities; universities, so the argument runs, are institutions which exist to further academic excellence, and therefore G.C.E. syllabuses have percolated downwards into the schools, always striving towards academic excellence, a goal not achievable by the majority of candidates. The breaking with the university tradition accelerated in the immediate post-war period, and a new examining body, the Associated Examining Board, (AEB), set itself the goal of breaking new ground by providing syllabuses in subjects which reflected the growing points in the curriculum, whatever the universities said. This was seen as a great liberating movement in the 'fifties and 'sixties. Considerable numbers of schools deserted the established G.C.E. boards and switched to A.E.B. Others, particularly secondary modern schools and further education establishments entering pupils for the first time for G.C.E., opted for the A.E.B., for an increasing number of subjects.
    But the greatest movement to liberate the schools from the constraints of the G.C.E. examination came with the establishment of the Certificate of Secondary Education in 1963, following the publication of the Beloe report and

SUBJECTS AND SYLLABUSES: THE NATIONAL CRITERIA

its acceptance by the government of the day. The philosophy of the C.S.E. was in many respects diametrically opposed to that of the G.C.E.: syllabuses were seen as tools giving the maximum opportunity for teachers to reflect the individual characteristics of their localities, their schools and their individual pupils. The boards were constituted on a regional basis to emphasise the need for close contact with schools, and the establishment of mode 2 and mode 3 procedures, whereby syllabuses were agreed by a group of schools, or submitted by an individual school, to be assessed externally in the case of mode 3, or with mode 3, by the school itself. Mode 3 thus represents the greatest freedom in the examination sphere - the school itself decides what should be taught and how it should be examined. The tremendous growth in the number of school initiated syllabuses reflected the great movement in the 'sixties towards diversity. The thousands of syllabuses examined by C.S.E. boards, not only provided examinations in the normal school subjects, but allowed scope for highly individual enterprises, some perhaps a little idiosyncratic. Unusual subjects such as navigation, took their place alongside film appreciation and media studies.

However, this heyday of the teachers' freedom to shape and determine both the content of syllabuses and methods of assessment lasted less than a decade. The C.S.E., boards and the schools they served, faced with the problems of attaining both acceptability and respectability, had to establish procedures which ensured comparability of standards and a clear understanding of what new subjects and syllabuses conveyed to the users of the system, especially the world of work. Furthermore, there had to be guarantees that school based syllabuses were properly taught, and internal examining and marking by the teachers, was fair, objective, accurate and unbiased. The challenge was met by establishing a detailed and rigorous network of moderation procedures administered by the boards. Many teachers who initiated mode 3 syllabuses in the 'sixties soon gave up, not only because of the enormous additional workload which this involved, but also because of the rigours of assessment. At Standing Conferences of the C.S.E. boards, arguments that it was more difficult to obtain high grades under mode 3 than under mode 1 found a place on early agendas and were often supported by the detailed statistical results for

SUBJECTS AND SYLLABUSES: THE NATIONAL CRITERIA

each mode and each subject which the boards publish annually.

The movement towards a unified system at 16+, resulting in common syllabuses and common assessment procedures, agreed by both the G.C.E. and C.S.E. boards, which characterised the 'seventies, reflected both compromise and consensus on the part of two distinct interests: the G.C.E. boards, whilst determined to maintain their reputation as the custodians of academic excellence, had to give ground in accepting that syllabus content, assessment components and grading schemes could not simply be based on their own models; the C.S.E. fraternity, for its part, had to abandon some of the notions of complete freedom for the individual teacher to determine syllabuses and marking schemes. The need was for agreed, joint examining at 16+. The growth in entries for the joint G.C.E./C.S.E. schemes at present operating, reflected the success of this consensus. It certainly proved attractive to the Secretary of State, Sir Keith Joseph, in giving serious consideration to harmonising the dual system, rather than merge it. In the end, harmonising reflected continuous compromise where radical reform was needed. Such reform is inherent in the emergence of G.C.S.E., and in particular, in its insistence on national criteria. The price to be paid for a common system of examinations in our secondary schools is the acceptance of a set of ground rules, laid down by the Department of Education and Science, administered and interpreted by the Secondary Examinations Council and influencing all syllabuses. How much of a constraint will national criteria prove to be? What are the ground rules and how will they affect the day to day life in the classrooms of the country?

The declared aim of G.C.S.E., is that pupils should be examined on what they know, understand and can do. To achieve this aim the intention is to provide as precise a list of rules as possible, covering the three interlinked concepts of each syllabus - content, assessment procedures and the grading system.

Much of the debate about the extent to which the government wishes to control the curriculum has centred on content, but national criteria concerns itself as much with general aims, principles and assessment procedures as it does with content. Indeed, many of the general principles laid down will be familiar to teachers, and are not always clearly distinguishable from the requirements set by

SUBJECTS AND SYLLABUSES: THE NATIONAL CRITERIA

examination bodies themselves. What is new is the setting down, almost in the form of tabloids, national rules, and the assumption by central government that it is the fount of all wisdom.

National criteria consists of one set of ground rules known as the general criteria, and another set, applying specifically to a number of subjects, designated subject specific criteria. The general criteria relates to all subjects and syllabuses to be examined.[1] It lays down the following ground rules:

1. Title
The title of a syllabus must clearly indicate both the content and the nature of the subject, distinguishing it clearly from other approved subject titles.
A specific requirement is laid down that there must be no 'undesirable proliferation' of titles, a theme which occurs throughout the criteria. There is a clear emphasis that the number of subjects to be examined should be reduced and the diversity of syllabuses at present being examined by the different boards should also be reduced.

2. Statement of aims.
It is laid down that each syllabus spells out in detail the educational aims which it seeks to attain.

3. Content and skills.
The body of knowledge, range of skills and understanding of the subject matter, need to be spelled out, but are coupled with the requirement that a syllabus should not be excessive in its demands. The theme of relating syllabuses to the specified educational aims recurs frequently, and there is a clear emphasis on the need to reduce overloading of syllabuses. This will certainly be welcomed by pupils and teachers.
The need for syllabuses to reflect the acquisition and development of skills is given equal rating with the acquisition of knowledge and understanding.

4. Assessment schemes.
A considerable proportion of the general criteria is taken up with detailed consideration of assessment procedures, to be considered in the next chapter. Here it is relevant to note that syllabuses are seen as normally offering appropriate combinations of board assessed and school assessed course

work. There is a clear expectation that the oral component and continuous assessment, two major features of C.S.E. examinations, should normally be present in all syllabuses, representing a powerful move in the C.S.E. direction. Whilst written papers retain their importance, they are no longer seen as the main or sometimes even the major element, of the new examining process. This has important implications for the day to day work in the classrooms - what is done throughout the last two years of compulsory schooling will often count as much as what happens during the final exam taken just before leaving school.

5. <u>Avoidance of bias and recognition of cultural diversity</u>.
The general criteria requests that efforts be made to ensure that syllabuses and examinations are free of political, ethnic and other forms of bias, and that they should bear in mind the linguistic and cultural diversity of society.

6. <u>Language</u>.
There is a specific requirement that the language used in examination papers should be clear, precise and easily understood by the candidates throughout the ability range. Examining groups are also asked to consider where and when special provision for candidates whose mother tongue is not English, should be made.

7. <u>Limited grade examinations</u>.
There is a recognition that examining groups should be prepared to set examinations from syllabuses where only a limited range of grades can be obtained, as is the case with many C.S.E mode 3 syllabuses at present. This is an important recognition that academically less able candidates should not only have access to the new examination, nor be put in a position of showing high failure rates. But such syllabuses could also serve abler candidates.

8. <u>Emphasis on relevance</u>.
The general criteria contains a statement that all syllabuses should show the relationship of the particular subjects to other study areas, to the candidate's own life, and should foster an awareness of economic, political, social and environmental factors. The general criteria then gives specific guidance on the format, content and presentation of syllabuses. These repeat to a

SUBJECTS AND SYLLABUSES: THE NATIONAL CRITERIA

considerable extent what is said in the earlier statements, but spell out in greater detail the assessment procedures to be considered in the next chapter. However, the emphasis on the requirement that there must be differentiation amongst candidates is a strong and recurrent theme throughout the criteria. There is insistence that differentiation should be achieved either by the use of differentiated papers, differentiated questions or differentiated components within questions or papers. It is this requirement which makes it clear that the G.C.S.E. is to be a common examination system rather than a common examination, an important and not always easily understood difference. The fine grading system reflects this philosophy of differentiation within a common framework, and it is this requirement which will present a real challenge to syllabuses aimed at mixed ability groups, where no such differentiation exists.

The Department of Education and Science insists that the national criteria are not 'intended to place a straight jacket on examination systems, or to stand in the way of new developments'.[2] The Secondary Examinations Council is required to act in consultation with the examination groups in keeping the national criteria under regular review to publish revisions and additions and is therefore, seen as the instrument of development and control. There is also the important proviso that whilst the criteria is seen to apply to all subjects examined within the G.C.E., arrangements also need to be made to exempt some of them from the national criteria themselves. There is thus the recognition that, however precise the list of rules, however careful the wording, there will be exceptions to the rule.

Teachers concerned with a curriculum which is largely subject based will need to study the subject related criteria to evaluate the extent to which they cause constraints on syllabuses. Such subjects specific criteria[3] exists for twenty subjects:-

English	science	craft, design &
mathematics	physics	technology
history	chemistry	computer studies
geography	biology	economics
religious studies	social science	business studies
French	Welsh	
art and design	music	classical subjects
		home economics

These of course, account for the majority of subject

SUBJECTS AND SYLLABUSES: THE NATIONAL CRITERIA

entries in the existing examinations, a trend which is likely to continue in G.C.S.E. However, it is important to note that all subjects not covered by the subject specific criteria published by the DES, need to submit proposals for syllabuses to the examining groups, who may themselves wish to adopt any additional requirements if they consider this necessary. There is an emphasis in the regulations that subjects for which no specific subject criteria have been published so far should not be considered less important.

An examination of the twenty subject specific criteria published reveal important differences. The criteria published for English, mathematics, biology, chemistry, physics, computer studies, French, craft, design & technology, music and classical subjects, are roughly equal in length and detail. However, those for science and curiously, home economics, go into considerably more detail, the science criteria being almost three times as long as the separate sciences. The same is true of home economics and both these subject areas reflect important and to some extent unresolved differences between the teachers and the Secretary of State. Subject teachers of these descriptions will need to study what may well prove controversial areas with great care.

Religious studies, business studies, art and design, geography and history, are dealt with in considerably less detail, the subject specific criteria taking up only half the space in the regulations, compared with the other subjects already mentioned, and economics and social science are despatched in three pages, almost as if the drafters had run out of energy or time. Even allowing for variations in syllabus content, these variations are significant because they already reflect the diversity of approach in a system geared towards uniformity. It is clear that the uniformity of approach, however much sought after, was simply not attainable in every case. It must of course be borne in mind that the national criteria themselves were drafted by the subject experts of the G.C.E. and C.S.E. boards under the auspices of a general council, set up specifically to do this job, and now dissolved. Its work was monitored by the D.E.S. with H.M.I's undoubtedly taking a hand, and the Secretary of State and his advisers clearly concerned themselves more with some subject areas than others. The resulting unevenness in the provision of subject specific criteria is

SUBJECTS AND SYLLABUSES: THE NATIONAL CRITERIA

thus clearly visible.

The subject specific criteria mentioned above require detailed studies by teachers, examiners and moderators. Although it can be assumed that a syllabus, once it has been approved by the examining group, and the Secondary Examinations Council, will be operational, the assessment and moderating procedures and, in particular, the need to maintain a close and detailed relationship between these procedures and the award of grades have pitfalls. The relationship between assessment techniques and grade descriptions is spelled out in detail and needs to be understood thoroughly by anyone contemplating the drafting of a mode 2 or 3 syllabus. A brief perusal of the subject specific criteria yields helpful information.

In English, two titles are to be used - English and English literature, and these are to be examined separately. The aims (common to both of them) are familiar to teachers of English:
(i)   to communicate accurately, appropriately and effectively in speech and writing;
(ii) to understand and respond imaginatively to what is heard, read and experienced;
(iii) to enjoy and appreciate the reading of literature;
(iv) for candidates to understand themselves and others.

These are then broken down into assessment objectives, which specify the need to understand, order and present ideas and opinions, to evaluate information in reading material and in other media, to show a sense of audience; to communicate effectively and appropriate in spoken English and to exercise adequate control of grammatical structures, sentence structure, punctuation and spelling.

The emphasis on oral communication is a central feature of the subject criteria. It is laid down specifically that oral communication is compulsory for all candidates in English, that it is to be separately assessed and appear as an endorsement of the certificate, using a different and shorter grade scale, i.e. a five-point numbered scale with grade 1 showing the highest and grade 5 showing the lowest level, as distinct from the seven point letter scale for the written examination. It is clearly stated that in order to obtain a grade in English, a candidate must attain at least a grade 5 in oral communication, alongside at least a grade G in the rest of the examination. Here, G.C.S.E. English clearly follows the C.S.E. pattern and abandons the purely written examination of the G.C.E. 'O' level approach. The criteria dealing with reading and writing are not significantly different from what is already common practice: candidates are expected to read literary texts, e.g. short stories, novels, autobiographies, poetry and prose; the section relating to writing simply distinguishes between 'closed situations' e.g. letters, report writing and open writing of a narrative, imaginative or personal nature. There is nothing new in this. Course work must account for at least 20% of all marks, and it is recognised that some examining groups will provide syllabuses assessed by course work only. Here again, we see the influence of the C.S.E. examination, and a distinct movement away from the idea of presenting candidates with written papers only. The need to provide differentiated assessment is again emphasised, seen in the suggestion that differentiated papers, differentiated tasks within course work, or a combination of such elements, with non-differentiated matter, should be available. However, there is no attempt to lay down the content of any syllabus.

The English literature subject criteria holds no surprise for either candidates or teachers. Acquiring first hand knowledge of literary texts and understanding them, recognising and appreciating the ways in which writers use language and achieve their effect and communicating a personal response to what is read, is the stock-in-trade of literature lessons. Whilst there is insistence on the detailed study of individual texts and recommendations on the wider reading of prose, poetry and drama, there is a specific statement that works for detailed study need not be prescribed in set texts and a wide personal choice is encouraged.

What emerges from a study of the subject criteria is a picture of a firm framework, laying down specific guidance in the form of procedures and principles, but not concerning itself with subject matter to be taught.

The subject criteria for mathematics is based to a considerable extent, on the Cockcroft Report on the teaching of mathematics in schools. Here, the statement that pupils 'should not be required to prepare for examinations which are not suited to their attainment, nor must these examinations be of a kind which will undermine the confidence of pupils' suggests a move away from much of what has loosely been described as traditional mathematics.

SUBJECTS AND SYLLABUSES: THE NATIONAL CRITERIA

Again, the aims of the criteria
(i) to develop mathematical knowledge and oral written and practical skills;
(ii) to read, write and talk about mathematics;
(iii) to develop a feel for numbers, to carry out calculations and understand the significance of the results, and
(iv) to apply mathematics to everyday situations, are the beginnings of a long list of general statements, which include the need to apply mathematics, particularly in science and technology, to appreciate the interdependence of different branches of the subject, and to lay a foundation for further studies. However, there is an important difference between this criteria and the previous one and the one for English. Whilst there is no requirement to include oral and practical work as part of the first examinations, for which preparations begin in 1986, there is a requirement that from 1988 to 1990, all examining groups must provide at least one syllabus which includes both oral and practical aspects, and that from 1990 onwards both these objectives must be included in all schemes. It is clear therefore, that the syllabuses which will get off the ground for 1986 will need to be amended again to respond to these requirements. Again, since oral examining in mathematics often features in mode 3 C.S.E. syllabuses, teachers of such syllabuses will be on home ground.

However, the mathematics criteria differs from many others because it contains clear references to content. This is seen as the core item of each syllabus and covers the four rules applied to numbers, to fractions, mathematical language, measures of weight, length, area, volume and capacity, time and other familiar material. The efficient use of calculators is specifically included.

The lists of topics contained in the mathematics criteria go into considerable detail and will therefore require careful checking by teachers. Whilst the majority of the material probably features in all mathematics syllabuses, the specific listing of areas to be studied, and skills to be attained, are presented with greater firmness than is the case with many other syllabuses. The other significant difference is that the criteria lists a large number of mathematical themes which constitute almost the whole of the syllabus for candidates expected to attain grades, E, F and G; to this list

SUBJECTS AND SYLLABUSES: THE NATIONAL CRITERIA

(list 1) is added another (list 2), listing further subject matter which must be included in any syllabus where candidates expect to obtain at least a grade C. This is the principle of prescribing a common core which everybody must study. Those aspiring to grades A or B are expected to have covered a syllabus in excess of the items listed, though here the examining groups are given a degree of discretion as to what to include. There is inherent in this approach some contradiction between the stated objectives in the general criteria, not to overload syllabuses and yet, in the mathematics subject criteria, doing precisely that! It is as if the enthusiasm to reform the teaching of mathematics shown by the Secretary of State in the proposed appointment of 350 special mathematics advisers, has run away with him. There is little doubt that even allowing for a considerable consensus among mathematics teachers as to what should be taught, the weight of material included in the 'common core' will cause difficulties, particularly at the lower ability end. This is likely to lead to the submission of a considerable number of mode 3 syllabuses with limited grades. However, even such syllabuses will have to contain at least part of the common core and may well lead to a rigidity of approach which many teachers will consider undesirable and many candidates difficult to digest. It is a reasonable forecast that the Secondary School Examinations Councils will find itself fairly early in the business of reviewing national criteria in this field.

Both the physics and biology subject criteria contain references to a common core, but much more modestly conceived than in the case of mathematics. In the case of physics, the core content deals with aspects of matter, energy, interactions, physical quantities and the application of physics, and there is a general statement that other topics were considered as part of a minimum core content, but not included because they were not regarded as essential to all syllabuses in physics. During the drafting stage there was a controversy between the Secretary of State and the teachers as to whether or not social and economic themes relating to physics should form part of any physics syllabus. The D.E.S., speaking for Sir Keith Joseph, wanted a largely 'practical' approach, with apparently little discussion of issues such as the development of nuclear physics and the risks facing the human race. Finally, the matter was resolved by agreeing that the technological application of social and economic interactions should be given due prominence, but that no examination questions should be set which did not require knowledge of the appropriate physics. The biology criteria follow a similar approach, listing a number of themes dealing largely with the diversity of organisms, their relationship with the environment, the maintenance of the individual, as part of the life process, forming a more modest core which should not cause undue difficulty. There is also some evidence of greater flexibility in these criteria as it allows aspects of biology, e.g. human biology and rural biology, as meeting the subject specific criteria. The situation is a little less happy in chemistry, where the core content is again spelt out in great detail, with suggestions as to how the core might be amplified. There is therefore a considerable risk of overloading in these syllabuses if the suggestions for amplification are taken too seriously.

The real problem of applying subject specific criteria to diverse approaches is reflected in the detailed publications relating to science and home economics. These have a prescriptive approach. In science, there is a forecast that further criteria are likely to be issued for agricultural science, astronomy and electronics, engineering science, in geology, horticulture, material science, rural science, and these are only some examples of the diversity of syllabus provision existing in science. In view of the obvious difficulty of finding common elements here, the criteria considers the arrangements of syllabuses in a number of sub-categories as follows: integrated, combined, united, associated and directed science. It then attempts to grapple with the problem of relating the subjects specific criteria to multiple award schemes, and states that science syllabuses in applied science, chemistry with biology, combined and environmental science, general science, integrated and material science, physical science, physical biology, physical chemistry, rural science and simply science, must all satisfy the general criteria. There are then a number of general statements which, although included in the subject specific criteria, are of an everyday nature, e.g. 'to develop abilities and skills that are useful in everyday life'. Finally, as if to realise the impossibility of the task of being too prescriptive in the face of such diversity, a number of specimen

SUBJECTS AND SYLLABUSES: THE NATIONAL CRITERIA

syllabuses are included, showing possible links between topics covering a particular theme. These include such wide ranging aspects as the study of photography, astronomy or, as a module, the use of water, which is based on a leaflet published by the Anglian Water Authority covering its responsibilities for rivers, water sewerage, drainage, conservation, recreation and could therefore, equally form the subject of a syllabus in geography or environmental studies. It remains to be seen whether the subjects specific criteria for science will reflect the diversity of provision clearly in use in the schools, or whether it will attempt to constrain the content to such an extent as to lead to the eventual disappearance of many syllabuses and the regression to the separate major sciences, where the prescriptive 'common core' approach has been established. It is likely that a battle may well lay ahead.

The subject criteria for home economics caused problems not dissimilar from those experienced with science but they seem to have been solved more successfully. Here, the definition of the subject by the Institute of Home Economists as 'A study of the inter-relationships between the provision of food, clothing, shelter and related services and man's physical, economic, social and asthetic needs in the context of the home' led the drafters of the subject criteria to define four major aspects as under-pinning all syllabuses. These were defined as family, food, home and textiles. These were to feature in all syllabuses. This led to immediate difficulties. In nearly all secondary schools there are distinct courses in home economics, many of which have bias towards the study of food and nutrition, and include a good deal of practical cookery; others owe their existence to the traditional teaching of needlework and embroidery, in recent years changed to the study of dress and textiles. Yet another distinctive area is centred on child development, now available both at '0' level and C.S.E., where the physical, social, intellectual and emotional development of young children are powerfully linked to a study of the family and parenthood, with an emphasis on the caring skills, with practical work involving the handling of young children. This latter area has been one of the most exciting and popular fields of study initiated by the C.S.E. boards in response to requests from schools. The Secretary of State appeared to insist that all aspects should feature

SUBJECTS AND SYLLABUSES: THE NATIONAL CRITERIA

equally in one and the same syllabus, but such an impossible request met with considerable opposition. Such a wide syllabus would have required at least double the present teaching time. The problem was finally solved by distinguishing between an area of main study and a common element. The common element was defined as
(i) human development, including physical, social and emotional development, according to age and sex;
(ii) health, including well being, including physical and psychological needs;
(iii) safety and protection;
(iv) efficiency, involving the management and working performances of materials, tools, equipment and the adjacent areas of the management of money and time, with value for money being mentioned specifically;
(v) a study of values, including personal and communal values;
(vi) asthetics, defined as the enhancement of the quality of life, through the enjoyment of food, textiles, and the home, and finally
(vii) the interaction with the environment, including the rights and responsibilities of consumers.

The main studies are to be drawn from the area of family, food, home and textiles. The subject criteria thus makes it possible to develop syllabuses with any of the following titles
    home economics
    child development
    home economics (food bias)
    home economics (textiles bias)
    home economics (home and the family).

The subject criteria moves somewhat uneasily between these four areas of study, insisting that all syllabuses must include a statement of the aims, concepts, specific details of the nature and range of skills to be taught and of the information to be given. There is a rigid requirement that the main study must account for sixty per cent and the common element for forty per cent of the marks, and a further requirement that not less than thirty and not more than fifty per cent must be allocated to assessment of practical work. The problem with this approach is that it can lead to rigidities, which are neither necessary nor desirable; however, the subject criteria contains examples of syllabuses with a particular bias; home maintenance, domestic heating, suitability of clothing.

SUBJECTS AND SYLLABUSES: THE NATIONAL CRITERIA

Pre-school child development and creative textiles form topics which are broken down into a number of content areas, skills to be taught and main concepts which relate to the topic. The notion of teaching and examining creative textiles may at first seem strange, but a careful study of the proposed themes suggest that what is required is an end product, and in that sense this topic does not differ markedly from existing provisions in dress and fashion syllabuses.

The remaining subject criteria are less complex. The French criteria is firmly based on the notion that it refers to the whole G.C.S.E. ability range and there is an expectation that a much greater number of candidates than at present will be entered, not only in French but in other modern languages. The common core of basic listening, basic reading and basic speaking, is spelt out only in general terms, and is accompanied by proposals on higher level reading, higher level speaking and higher level writing to provide for the more able pupils. In this area, mark allocation is left to the syllabus drafters, accompanied only by the general statement that it will depend on the differentiated test levels to be used and a recommendation between different levels. Apart from Welsh, no other subjects specific criteria for other modern languages are available so far.

The criteria for religious studies, which one might have expected to be controversial, are dealt with in a brief and straightforward manner. Language and concepts used in religion are ranged alongside a study of the place of religion in various communities, with scope for looking in rather more detail at least at one major world religion with buddhism, christianity, hinduism, islam, judaism and shikhism, being classified as world religions. Contemporary moral issues are to be dealt with by emphasising the need for understanding, and evaluating, on the basis of evidence and argument, issues of belief and practice, and there is no insistence on christianity, or any other religion, as the basis for a syllabus.

Although each examining group is required to provide at least one syllabus of the mode 1 type, concerned entirely with the study of christianity, the approach to content is flexible and allows considerable choice. Thus it is possible for a school to select any of the major world religions as a core element, the syllabus concerning itself with its origins and teachings, the history of the

33

religion, a study of sacred texts or a study of
traditions of a voluntary authority and relate this
to contemporary moral issues. Such a core element
may account for fifty per cent of the total marks,
the other fifty per cent being devoted either to
another major world religion studied similarly, and
thus allowing of comparative treatment, or of
allowing a deeper study of only one world religion,
using approaches different from those contained in
the core studies. Alternatively, a thematic study
of three major world religions is possible, centred
around themes such as the personality and
achievements of founders, religious leaders, sacred
writings, the nature of festivals, feast and solemn
days, a study of worship and ritual, an examination
of community life and personal experiences related
to aspects of moral teaching. The subject criteria
for religious education states quite specifically,
that candidates should be encouraged 'not only to be
aware of differences of opinion in matters of
religious belief and practice, but also to express
an opinion of their own, based on the use of
evidence and argument at a simple level.'[4]

Such an approach will commend itself to the
majority of teachers of religious education, who
have certainly succeeded in ensuring that the study
of the subject is progressively moving away from
didactic approaches and continues a welcome trend,
whereby secondary pupils are introduced to the
challenging and varying nature of religious beliefs.
Indeed, a study of the joint 'O' level/C.S.E.
examination in religious studies published by the
East Anglian/London Regional and University of
London School Examination Boards, to be first
examined in 1987, bears considerable resemblance to
the national criteria, so that schools taking this
particular syllabus should find little difficulty
in making what may only be minor adaptations to
conform with the criteria.

A similar approach is followed in history. Here,
the subject specific criteria encourages examining
groups to provide "a wide range of options to give
freedom to innovate and to reflect local interests.
It is therefore not desirable to stipulate a minimum
core of content".[5] Whilst there is again a
requirement that each examining group must offer at
least one syllabus which deals specifically with
historical phenomena relating to the intellectual,
cultural, technological and political growth of the
United Kingdom, there is a clear recognition that in
the case of history, a common core for all

SUBJECTS AND SYLLABUSES: THE NATIONAL CRITERIA

syllabuses is not suitable. Although examples drawn from syllabuses dealing with modern world history (1890 to the present day) Britain and Europe (1450 to 1600) British social and economic history (1760 - 1940) and a syllabus based on the Schools Council 13 - 16 history project, are given throughout the criteria, there is a welcome emphasis on freedom to choose content, allowing for variations in methodology. The statement that the course work component should carry a minimum of twenty per cent marks recognises the progress made since the introduction of C.S.E., moving away from the rigidity of setting papers with only a few questions and subject to time limitations.

The classical subjects are dealt with in a similar manner. Here, the criteria applies to subjects carrying the following titles: Latin, Greek, Roman civilisation, Greek civilisation, Latin and Roman civilisation and Greek civilisation, Classical civilisation, (Greek and Roman). A distinction is made between linguistic and non-linguistic subjects, but no specific recommendations with regard to content are made. Linguistic subjects are required to have a minimum core of content to enable candidates to understand unprepared prose passages and read at least two kinds of literature. In the case of the non-linguistic subjects, the wide diversity inherent in the study of the Classics is recognised by the specific statement that 'it is therefore inappropriate to stipulate a single minimum core of content'.[6] Syllabus drafters are required to state clearly the period and cultural area which form the main area of study; there is again considerable choice for teachers. The two examples stated, i.e. study of fifth century Athens, particularly concerned with the period 449 to 404 BC, and a study of Rome in the first century BC and the first century AD, with particular attention to certain topics such as social life, architecture and government, will cause no difficulty for teachers tackling what is an important minority area of the curriculum in many schools.

The criteria published for economics is one of the shortest, occupying only three pages. On this occasion, a core content is set out which must be included in all syllabuses entitled economics. The core relates to the basic terminology used in economics, differences between public and private sectors, the functioning of organisations and institutions such as trade unions and banks, trends

SUBJECTS AND SYLLABUSES: THE NATIONAL CRITERIA

and sequences in population growth, unemployment level, investment, inflation and national income, some reference to economic growth, entrepreneurship and basic economic theory. There is also reference to the inter-dependence of parts of the British economy with global trends, including some study of overseas trade, balance of payments and exchange rates. Most of these concepts are found in any economics syllabus. However, the allocation of marks between knowledge and understanding (maximum 40) and the application of such knowledge, analysis and judgment (minimum 60) is again rigid, compared with other schemes. There is also a requirement that data response questions must be included in all assessment schemes, either in the form of short answers such as multi-choice, or in continuous writing, and these must account for at least twenty per cent of the marks. There is a strong recommendation that data response and essay questions be set in a structured form. The course work component must carry a minimum of twenty per cent of the marks. The impression created by the criteria is that of a concise but somewhat rigid conception of the subject, with a possible risk of overloading the content.

    A similar approach is adopted in the criteria for business studies. Five major headings are identified to provide the core of the syllabus: external environment of the business, business structure and organisation, business behaviour, people in business, aiding and controlling business activity. Each component is sub-divided into further topics, stated as examples; thus, business structure and organisation deals with different types of organisations, reasons for specialisation, financial organisations, reasons for business growth, declining sources of finance for both revenue and capital, cash flow, returns on capital borrowing, taxation and budgeting control. These and other topics suggest a level of maturity and experience, which will not readily be found among 16 year olds, and the core is likely to prove too heavy to allow for other options in the syllabus. The fact that recall of knowledge requires a maximum of forty per cent of the marks, with application of knowledge, analysis and judgment a minimum of sixty per cent, again suggests a rigidity of approach which will not be welcomed by many teachers. However, the emphasis on data response questions and particularly on oral skills in assessing the work, may to some extent mitigate against an inherent rigidity, and the

SUBJECTS AND SYLLABUSES: THE NATIONAL CRITERIA

requirement that compulsory course work should attract not less than twenty, but not more than forty per cent of the marks available, is coupled with the suggestion that a project may lend itself to cross modular assignments. However, the kind of course work required is again spelt out in some detail, and is likely to prove a limitation on teachers who may wish to adapt that part of the syllabus to the more specific requirements of candidates in a locality. Whilst some options are available, this criteria, being confined to four pages, suggests that the drafters wanted to see the job done and did not perhaps devote the quality of thought which is shown in the approach to history.

The criteria in social science is more flexible. Although there is the requirement that the content should be based on specific themes, e.g. the social development of people, the process of income and wealth generation, the inter-relationship and inter-dependence of social, cultural, economic and political factors, the suggested themes allow varying interpretations and diversity in syllabus treatment. Some concepts likely to recur in any courses, such as power and authority, social differentiation and inequality, order and conflict, freedom and responsibility, are identified and there is a clear statement as to what students should know, understand and be able to handle at the end of the course. These requirements relate to social institutions and processes, politics and government, economic awareness and handling of data. Again, the assessment scheme sets out the weighting of skills as follows: Recall: twenty to thirty five per cent, organisation of work: twenty to thirty per cent, analysis: twenty to forty per cent, interpretations/evaluation/application: twenty to forty per cent. The now common requirement that course work should be included with a mark allocation between twenty and forty per cent, is stated, but on this occasion, there is a limitation. But course work carrying more than forty per cent of marks will only be accepted in exceptional cases. There is also a specific requirement that there must be an end of course written examination. Again, the criteria occupy only three pages, and again, there is the distinct impression that the drafters seem to be uncomfortable at the thought of allowing reasonable flexibility to teachers.

The criteria in art and design distinguishes between general courses based on various activities and use of media, and the more specialised courses

based on aspects of art. There is an immediate
recognition that there are a multiplicity of
approaches to both art and design, and that the
examining groups will wish to provide a wide choice
of options. No attempt is made to provide any
guidance on content. A useful distinction is made
in providing two forms of certification: art and
design unendorsed, where work may be submitted from
any broad area of study, or art and design endorsed,
where a single area of study is to be taken, say one
of drawing and painting, textiles, three dimensional
studies or photography. Schemes of assessment are
left flexible, including both course work and
controlled tests, with marking left to the
discretion of examining groups and schools. However,
it is envisaged that all syllabuses should include
at least two elements, i.e. course work and a test,
except in the case of external candidates. This
flexible approach to the criteria closely reflects
what is happening in schools, and no difficulty
should be experienced in the change to G.C.S.E.

A similar approach to art is followed in the
criteria for music. Whilst it is specified that
syllabus content should be closely defined and take
account of listening, performing and composing,
there is no attempt to specify content in detail.
Indeed, the need for a flexible approach is
recognised in the early stages of the document.
Music is seen as providing stimuli and experiences
for pupils throughout the ability range, including
those with special needs, and it is clearly stated
that the examination should reflect this diversity.
Assessment procedures relating to listening,
performing and composing, are based very largely on
existing practices with a generally liberal
approach. Thus, the recognition that all candidates
can listen and then respond to the same piece of
music, but show considerable variation in performing
and composing, is simply common sense, which has
found its way into a useful document.

Finally, two relatively new areas of study -
craft, design and technology and computer studies,
complete the publication of national criteria. For
C.D.T., a common core of skills and knowledge is set
out but again, there is much flexibility. Both the
design and making element is expected to feature in
all syllabuses, and there is a requirement that a
precise description of the work, which candidates
are expected to cover, must be stated. This
however, is inherent in the subject itself. The
requirement that the communication element

SUBJECTS AND SYLLABUSES: THE NATIONAL CRITERIA

should contain pictorial and free hand drawing, drawing to scale, use of colour, free hand work, and methods of lettering is based on well established practice in schools. The section on knowledge is sub-divided under control systems, energy, a study of materials and components and is brief and to the point. Finally, the criteria for computer studies has a longer section on core content, merging into the assessment objectives, requiring candidates to demonstrate knowledge and understanding of techniques to solve a variety of problems; in addition, pupils are expected to be able to use computers to produce solutions to appropriate problems and document these. The criteria sets out to provide a course of computer studies recognising the widespread use of computers and micro-processors at home, and the dynamic and developing nature of the subject. The recognition that computing dates rapidly is to be welcomed, and examining groups are asked to ensure that syllabuses remain appropriate and are brought up to date. Timed written papers and continuous assessment over a period of time both feature in the criteria, and it is understood that practical work in computer studies cannot be assessed in single sessions, but should be assessed over an extended period of time, under suitable conditions. Such an approach will be welcome by teachers as responding to the reality of the situation.

The vast number of subjects taught in schools and examined by boards for which no criteria has been published fall into two categories - those where such criteria will be issued by the D.E.S. at a later date, and those where the Secondary Examinations Council is expected to apply the principles of the criteria by sampling syllabuses. This will not prove too difficult with mode 1 syllabuses, but impossible with mode 3, which are likely to be left to the discretion of the examining groups.

There is no doubt that the whole concept of national criteria represents a powerful move by central government to influence and in a few cases, direct the content of the syllabuses. The freedom of the teachers to initiate and shape what is taught and how it is examined, which was such a strong feature of C.S.E. has been severely curtailed in the major subject areas - and this is the price the profession is asked to pay for the common examination system. But schools, teachers, pupils, and local education authorities show strong

individualistic trends, and are good at finding
their own solutions to problems caused by a
centralist approach. Some of the criteria reflect
this already; when the dust has settled, G.C.S.E.
may find itself in that midway position between the
great freedom of the 'sixties and the prescriptive
approach of the 'eighties, reflecting the
compromises which have served the schools well in
nearly a hundred years of public examinations.

Chapter Two

REFERENCES

(1) See DES publication G.C.S.E. 'General Criteria' HMSO 1985. Throughout this chapter, reference has been made to these ground rules as stated in the official publication, but variations and interpretations have been made to allow for comment.
(2) The G.C.S.E. - A General Introduction, DES paper, p.5. HMSO 1985.
(3) See Subject Specific Criteria published for the named subject by the DES, HMSO 1985, and circularised to all schools.
(4) G.C.S.E. - National Criteria - Religious Studies, p.2. DES publication, HMSO 1985.
(5) G.C.S.E. - National Criteria - History, p.2. DES publication, HMSO 1985.
(6) G.C.S.E. - National Criteria - Classical subjects p.2. DES publication, HMSO 1985.

Chapter Three

ASSESSMENT AND CERTIFICATION

The most important difference between the new
examination system and the present one, is that the
former is intended to be available for the great
majority of the school population. The combined
target group of the existing G.C.E. and C.S.E.
examinations covers some sixty per cent of secondary
school pupils, and it has long been a criticism of
the existing system that it splits the school
population. A unified, non-separatist comprehensive
school system, in the eyes of students, teachers,
parents and users, needs to have a similarly unified
examination system. Although comprehensive
schooling is over twenty years old, there have been
two separate public examination systems, an
arrangement unique to Britain and not easily
understood in other countries, where support for
comprehensive education is growing, where
separate school systems exist, but usually with a
single and relatively simple exam system, which is
easily understood if not always unchallenged.
G.C.E. syllabuses have continued to be designed
for the top twenty-five per cent of the school
population, and C.S.E. syllabuses for approximately
sixty per cent, including the G.C.E. sector. In
practice, this notion of a limited target group has
progressively disappeared. Schools have entered
a much larger proportion of pupils than sixty per
cent, particularly in the key subjects of English
and mathematics, but also in others. Because of the
unsuitability of many syllabuses for less able
pupils, a considerable number of mode 3 syllabuses
with limited grades have been submitted by schools
and accepted by the C.S.E. boards to fill a clearly
expressed need. The strains and stresses of
operating a dual system, with a cut-off point
limited to sixty per cent have been felt for many

years, and have prepared the ground for the present reform in exactly the same way the severe limitations of G.C.E. prepared the ground for the introduction of the C.S.E. examination twenty years ago. In the new system, there is a clear understanding that the examination should be available for a much wider range of candidates, covering almost the whole school population.

The standards required in the G.C.S.E. examination will be no less exacting than those required in the previous G.C.E. 'O' level and C.S.E. examination. 'O' level and C.S.E. taken together were originally designed for the upper sixty per cent of the ability range by subject. G.C.S.E. is not to be limited in that way. It will be designed not for any particular proportion of the ability range, but for all candidates, whatever their ability relative to other candidates, who are able to reach the standards required for the award of particular grades. Grade criteria are being developed for this purpose and will be incorporated into the subject criteria and syllabuses as soon as practical.[1] This is the government's statement for the general criteria for G.C.S.E., published by the Department of Education and Science in January 1985, and sets the stage for what is to come.

However, in making available the new system to practically the whole school population, there is a heavy emphasis on differentiation. The philosophy of differentiation permeates the whole of the general criteria, as well as the subject specific criteria which examination boards are expected to observe in accepting syllabuses. It is seen in the emphasis on questions on examination papers aimed at different target groups, on the structure and arrangements of examination questions, and in particular, in the proposed introduction of criteria referencing as distinct from norm referencing, to be discussed later. In this respect, the new system attempts to move secondary schools away from common approaches, common objectives and common goals towards a much more refined and highly differentiated system in schools. However, the emphasis on differentiated schemes and differentiated assessments is not imcompatible with mixed ability teaching. What will be required in the mixed ability situation is a much higher degree of individualised teaching, a much greater emphasis

ASSESSMENT AND CERTIFICATION

on individual tasks geared to the needs and abilities of the individual candidate, rather than common tasks applicable to a whole teaching group. The alternative to this approach is the organisation of specific target groups aimed at the achievement of particular grades inherent in the system of 'setting' (i.e. subject streaming). In practice, schools are likely to deal with the problem by encouraging a relatively high degree of overlap, rather than imposing rigid separation by setting. However, the challenge for both students and teachers, in meeting the new approaches should not be underestimated.

The new examination system provides for the needs of school students as well as post-school and adults. In stating specifically that there should be neither a minimum nor a maximum age for taking the new examination, the G.C.E. rather than the C.S.E. model is adopted, although the insistence on including substantial proportions of school based assessment follows the C.S.E. philosophy and practice. In order to meet the needs of post-school and adult students, examination boards are required to provide special syllabuses designated for external candidates who will be so described on their examination certificates.

The main components of assessment are spelt out in considerable detail in the general criteria and are reflected in the publications of the Secondary Examinations Council. First, there is the principle of 'fitness for purpose'. This spells out in detail the extent to which all parts of the examination, and the assessment procedures, should be related to the educational aims and the nature of the subject to be examined. The subject must be capable of being examined with validity and with an acceptable degree of reliability. Assessment schemes are required to reflect the assessment objectives stated at the beginning of syllabuses and to adhere to the allocation of marks envisaged. More specifically, assessment schemes should offer an appropriate combination of board and school assessed course work. This is a distinct break with the old system; G.C.E. examinations (although there have been some exceptions) are firmly wedded to the principle of written papers being taken at the end of the course and assessed externally. G.C.E. examinations, in some subjects, include elements of course work, but there has been no specific requirement that this should be the case - the general rule is the written paper at the end of a course of study. The insistence that school based assessment should be part of the new examination is, on the one hand, a recognition of the success of this method of examining by the C.S.E. sector, and on the other, a distinct and important move away from the philosophy of purely external examining. Indeed, the national criteria sees teacher judgment as a highly important component: assessment by the candidate's teacher is fundamental to the use of course work in examinations.

"The candidate's teacher is the only person who can take into full account the candidates personal contribution to the work which is being assessed and the extent of any assistance from the teacher or other outside sources. Consequently the teacher is likely to be in the best position to judge the merits of his or her own candidates in relation to each other," so says the general criteria published by the D.E.S. in January 1985. [2]

A second and highly important difference between the existing and the new system is the new requirement to relate examination processes to resource provision. Whilst it may be argued that this is already the case and is reflected in the fee structure of the examining boards, the designs of all examination papers and procedures have been based on the philosophy that the job needs to be done, paid for, and that schools, candidates and local authorities must find the money, and the time. G.C.S.E. states specifically that schemes of assessment must not make unreasonable demands on candidates, either with regard to the amount of time devoted to examining as such, and in the requirements for course work to be done. There is an explicit statement that neither a syllabus nor a scheme of assessment may make unreasonable demands on human and financial resources. Whilst there may be considerable discussion as to what constitutes unreasonable demands, teachers who have both initiated and implemented the C.S.E. examinations know that this has been done on the basis of a vast amount of voluntary work, both within and beyond the classroom. The design of syllabuses to fit particular target groups to accommodate the needs of schools, reflected particularly in the inclusion of course work, substantial oral examinings in subjects beyond foreign languages, thousands of mode 3 syllabuses and the operation of an administrative system involving a high degree of teacher participation, all have resource implications. If we add up the work done by thousands of examiners for both G.C.E. and C.S.E. examinations, outside school hours, and often demanding the use of supply teachers, it is clear that the present system never envisaged the present economic climate, the impact of cuts on the education service, and the increasing strains and stresses felt in secondary schools for a variety of reasons, not least the turbulence of present times. In the early stages of introducing G.C.S.E., pressures are likely to be felt very intensely; however, once the new system has settled down, resources needed for examining could be managed both more effectively and efficiently provided there is a sufficiently high level of investment at the start. It is therefore necessary to distinguish between the growing pains and present difficult situations giving rise to considerable controversy in the short run, but capable of solutions once the right combination of school based and external procedures has been achieved.

The approach to schemes of assessment as laid down in the general criteria make reference to prohibited subject combinations, to the avoidance and bias and recognition of cultural diversity; the language to be used in papers should be clear, precise and intelligible to the candidates, and there should be a relationship between the subject to be examined to other areas of study; what is being examined and assessed should be relevant to the candidate's personal life. It is also stressed that there should be an awareness of the economic, political, social, and environmental factors. Much of this is of course, already the case in existing G.C.E. and C.S.E. syllabuses, and the statement is therefore a recognition of the best practices. However, the emphasis on maintaining and where necessary initating such approaches, is new. Bearing in mind that the vast majority of syllabuses will have a school based component which will carry at least twenty per cent, and in some cases, a hundred per cent of all marks allocated, the means of externally moderating school based assessment are spelt out in considerable detail in the general criteria. First, there is the requirement that the initial syllabus submission must state in detail the nature and extent of school based examinations, whether initiated by the school or by the examining board. The criteria for the inclusion of such internally assessed components are spelt out clearly:
(i) to assess objectives which cannot be assessed

externally;
(ii) to assess objectives which are different from those applied to purely written examinations;
(iii) to complement the assessment of the written component; and
(iv) to assess objectives for which other forms of evidence are difficult to obtain, e.g. such as the skill in practical cookery.[3]

Examining techniques are defined as scrutinising, monitoring and moderating throughout the examining process. These approaches are of course, well known and well tried and do not represent a significant change in what already happens. The moderation of work by moderators, inspection either by looking at samples of work or examining the projects of a whole group, and relating the marks awarded to similar groups in other schools in order to maintain comparability of standards, are nothing new. Statistical moderation is seen as a supplementary method, but in concept is downgraded from present practice:'Statistical moderation may therefore be used only if the relationship between the performance of groups of candidates on the internally assessed and the externally assessed components is such as to justify its use'; and again, 'Statistical moderation must not be applied in a purely mechnical way, but any scheme of statistical moderation must include provision for its operation, to be monitored by some form of personal inspection which involves the power to override the statistical operation under suitable safeguards and subject to the general criteria specified......'[4] Such requirements form an important break with a tradition of examining which has relied heavily on the statistical method. Although instructions to examiners derive from agreed marking schemes, the general acceptance of the principle that the performance of candidates, needs to be related to broad categories, expressed by a percentage of candidates securing certain grades has never been seriously questioned. Indeed, where performances of candidates have been either substantially below or above what may have been expected, the adjustment of marks to conform to previous expectations is a technique used both in external and internal school examinations. It is seen more frequently in internal examining, when marks sometimes have to be 'scaled' if a paper proves too easy, or too difficult, causing a 'bunching' of the performances round a narrow range of percentages or grades. The shift away from pre-conceived expectations as reflected in the comments on use of the statistical method, is an important change, but needs to be seen in relation to the kind of decision required in determining which grades should be awarded. The methods by which the grades are to be arrived at are highly important and not a little controversial.

One of the most controversial aspects of the new system and likely to be subject to further challenges and possible modifications is the introduction of a seven-point <u>grading scheme</u>. This is an extension of the present five point scheme used by both the 'O' level and the C.S.E. boards. The relationship between the existing and the new system as far as grades are concerned, is reflected in the following table:[5]

G.C.E. 'O' level	G.C.S.E.	C.S.E.
A	A)	
B	B)	1
C	C)	
D	D	2
E	E	3
	F	4
	G	5

The use of a seven point scheme has been criticised in many quarters, certainly by some of the teachers' associations, and notably the N.U.T., but also by some employers who have stated that such a refined and highly differentiated scheme is unnecessary for their recruitment purposes.
Teachers who come face to face with examination candidates, and who have to grapple with sometimes negative attitudes caused by the expectation of low grades, have been sharply critical of a system which envisages a substantial proportion of the school population obtaining grades F or G, with an ungraded performance below the bottom grade G. It is with regard to the grading system that major criticisms have emerged - they are that the Secretary of State has sought to maintain fundamental elements of the old system while introducing a new one, and has produced what many users will see as an unnecessary complication at best, or an absurdity at worst. Although the equivalence between C.S.E. Grade 1 and Grades A, B and C G.C.E. 'O' level is a firmly established feature of the present system, with C.S.E. 1 being widely accepted, there has been no equivalence between the lower D and E grades of 'O' level, and C.S.E. grades 2 and 3. Indeed, the

ASSESSMENT AND CERTIFICATION

monitoring of 16+ joint examinations have sometimes thrown up evidence which has pointed the other way, with candidates graded 2 or even 3 at C.S.E. obtaining an 'O' level pass Grade C. The seven point grading system is therefore a distinct disadvantage, likely to meet with unfavourable reactions from both examiners and examined, with disenchantment once its full significance is appreciated. There is no doubt that pressure will build up in the coming years to modify the system and return to a five point scale. In the meantime, the 'O' level boards are charged with the responsibility of maintaining the standard of grades A to C, with C.S.E. boards exercising corresponding responsibility for grades D to G.

This too is an uneasy and probably an unworkable compromise. The new examining groups are an amalgamation of 'O' level and C.S.E. boards, and the teachers who are drafting syllabuses, determining methods of assessments, and applying both the general and subjects specific criteria, come from schools which teach candidates taking both the G.C.E. and the C.S.E. examinations. This difference is therefore artificial and not reflected in the day to day work of the examining boards. The exercise of this responsibility on a separatist basis is at best a temporary device, the reason for which is not readily apparent except in a political sense. The approach to such a refined grading system is further reflected in the proposals to introduce distinction and merit certificates, which are at present under discussion. Consultations on this are proceeding, but the Secretary of State's proposals are that distinction certificates should be awarded to candidates who achieve at least two grades A and not more than one grade C over seven subjects which are identified as follows:

(i) mathematics;
(ii) English;
(iii) a science;
(iv) a modern language;
(v) one from history or geography;
(vi) one from craft, design and technology, home economics, art and design, and music;
(vii) one from another science, another modern language, the other subjects from groups (v) or (vi) i.e. English literature, Welsh, religious studies, classical subjects, additional mathematics, economics, business or social studies, computer studies.

With regard to the merit certificates, two

possible models are under consideration: one is a reduction of what is demanded for the distinction certificates by requiring given grades in six rather than seven subject areas, similar to those already spelled out. An alternative model would require seven subjects, but grade requirements which are less demanding, i.e. four average grades of C or better, with not more than one grade D from a group of subjects, and no grade D below the seven subjects quoted. These proposals have ran into a storm of criticism throughout the teaching profession, both on the grounds that the grading scheme as envisaged, already has an inbuilt mechanism showing distinction (any pupils achieving high grades in a number of subjects achieve such distinction), and because of the likely backlash on the curriculum and even the possibility that this would be distorted for many pupils. The Cambridge Examination Syndicate has carried out an investigation showing the possible effect of the introduction of distinction certificates, using the 1984 ordinary 'O' level examinations as a base for a forward projection. The Cambridge Syndicate makes the point that with freedom of choice, candidates entering for the examinations of more than one group, (it is not uncommon in some schools to select subjects from different boards), would find themselves ineligible for the award of a distinction certificate unless this becomes a national certificate based on all results obtained. The Syndicate then offers to service such a co-ordinating body or central agency. At the time of writing consultations are proceeding but no decision has been reached.

But a much more fundamental and important reform is the envisaged change from norm reference to criteria related grades. This is a new concept in examining, and is fundamental to an understanding of the changes which are envisaged.

The present system of awarding grades is described as norm referenced because it is based on the assumption that the number of candidates taking either the G.C.E. or C.S.E. examination will achieve results which are broadly similar year by year, and correspond approximately to candidates across the ability range from which the candidates are drawn. The examination boards each year publish the percentage passes for each subject and each grade, and although there are variations both within subjects and examining boards which are quite considerable, this notion of norm referencing is

ASSESSMENT AND CERTIFICATION

firmly established.
    These percentage tables, showing different grades awarded by the various examining boards are closely studied by heads, senior teachers and departmental heads who make the decisions as to which examining boards they use. There are many discussions and speculations in countless school staffrooms as to which papers of which examination boards are easier, or more difficult, and switches are made accordingly. The system of norm referencing - the norm being what is expected in advance of the examination - is firmly entrenched. The C.S.E. boards collage their statistics nationally, so that regional variations are shown up sharply when percentages are compared across the country. The assumption is of course, that there needs to be at least some similarity between the number of candidates obtaining the various grades, wherever they go to school; whilst it is accepted that there may be considerable differences, where such differences emerge reasons are sought and need to be given. Criteria related referencing seeks to sweep away this system and substitutes an entirely new assessment technique, based on the notion that a grade should be defined precisely and that the criteria relating to the award of such a grade should apply to the individual candidate only, without reference to or regard to norms extending to other groups of candidates. The components determining the award of a certain grade are stated with considerable precision both in the general and in the subjects specific criteria. The following principles determine this process:

(i)   grade criteria defines the main area of knowledge and understanding;
(ii)   grade criteria specifies the main skills and competences to be tested within each subject;
(iii)   therefore, skills, knowledge and understanding need to be defined and related to each grade.

Examining boards are required to prepare for a change from the present system towards grade related criteria within the next few years. In the meantime, and in preparation for the new system, grades C and F are seen as the main reference grades in G.C.S.E., and a study of the application of the new grades in two or three subject areas shows the movement towards the change. History, craft design and technology,[6] and mathematics have been selected as examples, but similar approaches are followed in

51

ASSESSMENT AND CERTIFICATION

other subjects.
In history, candidates obtaining a grade F are expected

6.1.1. to recall and display a limited amount of accurate and relevant historical knowledge: to show a basic understanding of the historical concepts of cause and consequence, continuity and change, sufficiently supported by obvious examples; to identify and list differences and similarities;

6.1.2. to display knowledge of perspectives of other people based on specific examples of situations and events;

6.1.3. to show ability to comprehend straight-forward evidence; to extract partial and/or generalised information;

6.1.4. to demonstrate the obvious limitations of a particular piece of evidence; to list some of the evidence needed to reconstruct a given historical event;

6.1.5. to make simple comparisons between pieces of evidence; to list the major features of two or more pieces of evidence without drawing conclusions from it;

6.1.6. to communicate in an understandable form; to use simple historical terminology.

For grade C, the following requirements are laid down: Candidates will be expected

6.2.1. to recall and use historical knowledge accurately and relevantly in support of a logical and evaluative argument; to distinguish between cause and occasion of an event; to show that change in History is not necessarily linear or 'progressive'; to compare and contrast people, events, issues and institutions; to demonstrate understanding of such concepts by deploying accurate though limited evidence;

6.2.2. to show an ability to look at events and issues from the perspective of other people in the past; to understand the importance of looking for motives;

6.2.3. to demonstrate comprehension of a range of evidence either by translating from one form to another e.g. explaining accurately and fully questions demanding specific information to be extracted from the evidence;

6.2.4. to demonstrate the limitations

of a particular piece of evidence; e.g. point to the use of emotive language and to generalisations based on little or no evidence; to indicate the other types of evidence that the historian would need to consult in relation to the topic and period in question;

6.2.5. to compare and contrast two or more different types of evidence and write a coherent conclusion based on them, though all aspects may not be taken into account;

6.2.6. to communicate clearly in a substantially accurate manner, making correct and appropriate use of historical terminology.

The difference in what is expected from a grade C and a grade F candidate are thus clearly visible. Clearly, such a system of establishing criteria has the advantage that superficial or subjective marking of scripts is much less likely to happen than at present. However, no one should be under the illusion that the degree of exactitude spelled out here will automatically be applied by examiners accustomed to and trained in other methods. The application of criteria reflected in grade C, and even more so in the higher grades, require that the examiner must not only bear in mind, but refer closely and frequently to each individual script, to ensure that he or she keeps within the criteria reference. In the early stages such an approach is likely to require considerably more time than has been available for completing and marking scripts and publishing the results. In a subject such as history, the time involved in applying the grade descriptions will be quite considerable.

In craft, design technology grades C and F are spelled out in a somewhat different way, the emphasis being on skills.

Grade C - C.D.T.

9.2. Skills
1 Design
The candidate will have identified a problem and made a clear statement of the design brief. Investigation and analysis of the most important aspects will have led to the generation of a range of ideas as possible solutions to the problem. There will have been some evidence of first hand collection of relevant information and an application of knowledge of materials, components and constructions. The

ASSESSMENT AND CERTIFICATION

candidate's powers of discrimination will have enabled reasons to be given for the selection/rejection of those details considered in arriving at a preferred solution, and a valid evaluation will have been made on the basis simple criteria.
2   Making
The candidate will have shown evidence of good workmanship and sound construction in the material(s) used. When an artefact was realised, fitting parts will have located well, the finished item will have been constructionally sound and functional. Where appropriate, suitable finishing techniques will have been used and 'finishes' will have been successfully applied.
3   Communication
The candidate will have demonstrated a range of communication skills sufficient to initiate and develop ideas and to convey them to others. He will have written a factual and accurate report, shown oral competency and been able to use freehand and other graphical techniques. In Design and Communication examinations he will have applied graphic techniques to unfamiliar situations, shown an understanding of conventions and displayed qualities of draughtsmanship.
9.3. Knowledge
This will have reflected an understanding of technical and scientific principles, materials, components, constructions, tools and machines sufficient to solve problems and realise solutions which meet identified criteria. Knowledge of processes will have enabled sufficient planning and sequencing to ensure that work was effectively carried out to a good standard. A sound understanding of safety requirements will have been shown together with an awareness of the need for conservation of energy and other resources. A knowledge of principles and conventions used in graphic communication will have enabled the production of work to current standard practice.
GRADE F
9.4. Skills
1   Design
The candidate will have made a limited investigation of a problem posed by others

ASSESSMENT AND CERTIFICATION

and adopted by him. He will have listed the main features without a detailed analysis but may have collected relevant information from one source. Only one possible solution will usually have been offered although there may have been simple variations suggested and any evaluation will have been in the light of one or two elementary criteria. Some appreciation will have been shown related to the choice of materials, constructions and components with reasons or observations related to choice in at least one area.

2 Making

The candidate will have demonstrated limited manipulative skills with at least one material but these will not have been of the order to enable him to avoid difficulties with constructional operations. When an artefact was realised, fitting parts will have located adequately and the solution will have been functional. Where appropriate, there will have been evidence of the use of a suitable finish.

3 Communication

The candidate's oral and written communication will have been restricted and his graphic skills limited. Incomplete or poor drawings will have shown some of the information required for making an artefact or control system, and there are likely to have been only a few dimensions. In design and communication examinations the ability to use graphic techniques will have been greater and will have demonstrated the ability to use the more important conventions.

9.5. Knowledge

This will, in the main, have been superficial and the understanding of technical and scientific principles, materials, components, constructions, tools and machines will have been limited in breadth. The candidate will have stated the important properties of some materials or had a more detailed knowledge of one and been able to apply$_8$ this to appropriate common uses.

In this area of the curriculum, the change from norm referencing to criteria referencing is likely to be achieved more smoothly and more quickly. First, the teachers concerned will already have become accustomed to making individual judgments and assessments based on skills as demonstrated in processes within a workshop or drawing office, or in the quality of design and communication as shown in the finished article, and second, because the relationship between a body of knowledge and its application to techniques requiring particular skills is already firmly established. However, a close perusal of the grade descriptions also shows that the approach to differential assessment is rather more flexible than in history. To say that a candidate who obtains a grade C will have identified a problem and made a clear statement of the design brief, whereas one obtaining a grade F will have made a limited investigation of such a problem supplied by others, does not establish the extent to which teacher help is available even to the grade C candidate. Similarly, the distinction between an understanding of technical and scientific principles covering material components, constructions, tools and machines, for the grade C candidate, and what is stated as a superficial understanding of largely the same areas, may not in practice, be capable of the fine distinction envisaged. This all points to the need for a serious re-assessment of a grading system which in practice may well be too highly differentiated to stand up to day to day usage.

With regard to mathematics, the subject specific criteria are stated as forming "a minimum list of qualities, abilities and skills, and the weight attached to each of these may vary for different levels of assessment within a differentiated system".

There follows a long list of requirements - seventeen in all, of which the first six are quoted to indicate the flavour of the criteria:
3.1. recall, apply and interpret mathematical knowledge in the context of everyday situations;
3.2. set out mathematical work, including the solution of problems, in a logical and clear form using appropriate symbols and terminology;
3.3. organise, interpret and present information accurately in written, tabular, graphical and diagrammatic forms;
3.4. perform calculations by suitable methods;
3.5. use an electronic calculator;
3.6. understand systems of measurement in everyday use and make use of them in the solution of problems;

The criteria then states specifically that the objectives can only be achieved by assessing work of candidates done <u>in addition</u> to time limited

ASSESSMENT AND CERTIFICATION

examinations, and orders examining groups to include at least one scheme to provide an <u>oral</u> examination based on answering questions on mathematical ideas involving mental calculations, and <u>practical</u> components based on 'extended pieces of work'. At least one such scheme must be provided by all groups between 1988 and 1990, and from 1991, all mathematics schemes must contain both the oral and practical component.

There follows long lists of mathematical notions processes, skills which are spelled out in considerable detail. Whilst such details are not uncommon in well designed mathematical syllabuses, the range of tasks to be performed, the exactitude with which given tasks are to be achieved, and the variation in depth of treatment, must mean that a considerable degree of flexibility will have to be allowed in relating the assessment objectives to the grades.

However, even given such flexibility, there is a stony road ahead for both candidates and teachers in translating a particular procedure into practice, and the criteria drafters at least recognise that the envisaged exactitude may have to be subject to modification:

> "grade descriptions are provided to give a general indication of the standards of achievement likely to have been shown by candidates awarded particular grades. The grade awarded will depend in practice upon the extent to which the candidate has met the assessment objectives overall, and it might conceal weakness in one aspect of the examination which is balanced 9
> by the above average performance in some other".

The now customary lists are then related to both grades F and grade C, as in other subject areas. Here, the examples stated are worth quoting in full, as they indicate both the range, complexity and treatment of similar subject areas for higher ability candidates (grade C) and for those expected to achieve an average performance (grade F).

Grade Descriptions

Assessment Objective	Grade F examples	Grade C examples
3.3.	Extract information from timetables. Tabulate numerical data to find the frequency of given scroes. Draw a bar chart. Plot given points. Read a	Construct a pie chart from simple data. Plot the graph of a linear function. travel graph.

57

ASSESSMENT AND CERTIFICATION

3.4. Add, subtract and multiply integers. Add and subtract money and simple fractions without a calculator. Calculate a simple percentage of a given sum of money.

3.5. Perform the four rules on positive integers and decimal fractions (one operation only). Convert a fraction to a decimal.

3.6. Measure length, weight and capacity using metric units. Understand relationships between mm, cm, m, km; g, kg.

3.7. Perform a money calculation with a calculator and express the answer to the nearest penny.

3.8. Draw a triangle given three sides. Measure a given angle.

3.9. Continue a straightforward pattern or number sequence.

3.10. Use simple formulae, e.g. gross wage = wage per hour x number of hours worked, and use of A = l x b to find the area of a rectangle.

3.11. Recognise and name simple plane figures and common solid shapes. Find the perimeter and area of a rectangle. Find the volume of a cuboid.

Apply the four rules of number to integers and vulgar and decimal fractions without a calculator. Calculate percentage change.
Perform calculations involving several operations, including negative numbers.

Use area and volume units.

Given a reasonable approximation to a calculator calculation involving the four rules.
Use a scale drawing to solve a two-dimensional problem.
Recognise, and in simple cases formulate, rules for generating a pattern or sequence.
Solve simple linear equations. Transform simple formulae. Substitute numbers in a formula and evaluate the remaining term.
Calculate the length of the third side of a right-angled triangle. Find the angle in a right-angled triangle, given two sides.

In schemes of assessment where the objective is applicable:

3.17. Carry out a simple survey; obtain straight-

Investigate and describe the relation-

forward results from the   ship between the sur-
information obtained.   face area and volume
                             of a selection of
                             solid shapes. $_{10}$

Finally, we need to examine the envisaged change in the whole assessment system from norm to criteria referencing, a formidable technical task, wisely left for later, when the common system has established itself firmly.

The philosophy underlying the switch from norm referencing to criterion referencing needs to be clearly understood by teachers and others who have to communicate this change to students, parents, employers and all others concerned with the examination. First, there is the desire that what constitutes a grade should be communicated more clearly and in greater detail to all concerned, and this is readily understood and accepted.

Second, there is the intention that students should be more highly motivated by knowing in advance, and with greater precision than is the case at present, what is expected from them. This too, is likely to be an advance on the present situation where the award of a particular grade is often shrouded in mystery, and sometimes leads to considerable dismay especially when candidates with a good school record fail to perform adequately in an examination rigidly limited to a time scale. However, against this must be set the possibility that candidates of more limited ability, may see the achievement of a higher grade as something completely beyond their reach, whereas under the present system this need not be the case. The real problems of changing from norm to criterion referencing are however, not merely problems of technique and training. They relate to the clearly expressed desire to break an established tradition in examining across the whole range of subjects taught in schools.

First and foremost, there is the challenge to the established principle that the 'one off' system of examining candidates and awarding them a grade on the basis of a written performance in say a two hour paper, needs to be abandoned, and phased assessment must become part of the examining process. Added to this is a high degree of precisions set out in the proposals, reflecting a mathematical mind, and certainly influenced by the Cockcroft Report and its author. This precision combines with a philosophy of 'tidying up' the whole system, which however cannot be applied to those subjects where exactitude of expression are only one element in demonstrating the quality of the performance. Thus, exactitude in performing well in mathematics or physics is relatively easily identified if the outcome corresponds reasonably closely to the assessment objectives. The same principle cannot be applied in the broad range of art subjects, which will inevitably have larger elements of subjectivity than the sciences.

Finally, there is inherent in the philosophy of criteria referencing also the philosophy underlying the use of graded tests. This sees testing as progressive task orientated, closely linked to the learning process. It is of course, well known and used in music examinations, and in the more recently introduced graded tests used in foreign languages. A graded test scheme consists of a number of tests which become progressively more difficult, more complex and are taken by the students only when there is a high likelihood of success. There are no options and the tasks to be achieved are well known both by teachers and pupils in advance. A further component of the philosophy of criteria referencing is the desire not only to record the achievements of pupils, but also, to some extent, provide a simple profile, thus linking the notion of records of achievement with profiling. Whilst all such processes are inter-related, they are nevertheless different. Popham, in his book 'Criterion Referenced Measurement' [11] defines the characteristics of a criterion reference test as follows:
(i)   An unambiguous descriptive scheme;
(ii) an adequate number of items per measured behaviour;
(iii) sufficiently limited focus;
(iv) reliability;
(v)   validity;
(vi) comparative test data.

G.C.S.E., by having to employ both general and specific criteria, goes a long way towards the first objective, and by linking grades to specific skills and understanding also attempts to limit focus. However, such notions are so different from the system of examining pupils based on aggregating marks which seek to measure in a much more general way, areas of knowledge, certain skills and abilities to communicate readily in writing. There is some risk that criteria referencing will cause confusion. Serious consideration will therefore need to be given to simplifying the whole notion if it is to get off the ground. One criticism which has been made of the new examination system is that it introduces too much too soon and too quickly. Knowing the long history of discussion and controversy which preceded the establishment of a common system, this may not be immediately apparent, but there is a world of difference between moving forward in a situation where existing 16+ schemes were based on consensus, common practice, and commonly designed syllabuses based on an existing grading system, and what is now envisaged. The requirement for syllabuses to conform to national criteria both in a general and specific sense, coupled with the introduction of grade related criteria, in a seven point grading system, set against the resource crisis which afflicts all state schools, must mean that severe strains and stresses will be felt in the new system, which can be reduced by careful phasing, staging and training. It is therefore to be welcomed that criteria referencing will be introduced at a later stage and not at the same time as the first examinations to be held in 1988. What is needed is a simplified, rather than a sophisticated approach, a chance for the system to get off the ground and settle down, accepting that there will be imperfections, but concentrating on the growing points and successes. There is a risk that undue emphasis on perfect techniques, on the imposition of special requirements in too many cases and a general pre-occupation with national criteria could lead to a considerable disenchantment and resistance to a much needed reform. The Secondary Schools Examinations Council, the examining groups and not least, the Department of Education and Science will need to understand the complexities, and be sympathetic to the difficulties in getting the new system off the ground in the schools. What will be required is not simply a monitoring of the application of national and general criteria from above, and the implementation of new techniques, but an understanding that there are already signs of powerful moves away from external examining which could prove attractive to both schools and the users of the system. Here, three trends are clearly visible:

(i) The ascendancy of profiling and records of achievement is a powerful and dynamic force within the school system, and does not rely on G.C.S.E., as such, or similar externally administered systems. Whilst still in its early stages, the attraction of recording achievements of pupils in areas not only within, but beyond normal classroom experience, is considerable and could be very rewarding. If the curriculum is conceived not merely as a collection of subjects, but as the totality of all activities and processes contributing to the development of the young person, a very different approach emerges. It could be more meaningful to a school leaver to take away a record of achievement, which records a totality of tasks, involvement in school life and beyond, and contributions made, reducing the importance of examination grades, however carefully defined and referenced. In a new political situation, teachers may be more willing than at present to pioneer such developments extensively. If personal qualities and attitudes are also documented as part of the profiles which already exist in many schools, the attraction of assessments perceived as different from the new examination system could prove considerable.

(ii) The graded test movement is likely to gain in ascendancy. It is simple, easily understood and provides targets not subjected to national or any other officially controlled criteria. If the whole machinery of examining becomes too elaborate, the stresses and strains in launching G.C.S.E., the sheer burden of coping with its complexities could lead to its rejection. The graded test movement suffers no such disadvantages and may well develop without becoming part of the new system, and could eventually replace it, alongside developing records of achievement and profiles.

(iii) The impact of the new technical and vocational initiative, the emphasis on pre-vocational elements in secondary education, and the use of assessment models which owe more to notions of vocational training as seen in further education, than the broad concept of school based assessments, are a force to be reckoned with. There is therefore, the distinct possibility that the new examination system, however well designed and advantageous over the old, may itself be subject to considerable modification as we approach the turn of the century.

However, the next few years will surely see G.C.S.E. launched.

The new examining groups will award G.C.S.E. certificates, which will state the names of the examining boards within the group, the grades applicable to each subject, and the statements already mentioned relating to each of the new different grades. The certificates will be counter-signed on behalf of the Secretary of State for Education and Science, or in the case of Wales, the Secretary of State for Wales. It is expected that the examinations will take place during the summer term as at present, with the major impact of examining felt after Whitsun, as is the case with G.C.E. This will clearly shorten the examination season and allow more time for teaching, although practical examinations, and particularly the impact of considerable additional oral examining will have to be translated into timetable schedules. The examining groups are responsible for publishing the results, and are expected to agree on a range of dates when this should take place. A good way of coping with orals, practical examinations, written papers and the many tasks to be performed will be to collapse all secondary school timetables at Whitsun, a procedure already followed in many schools. Most examinations could then be accommodated in the last few weeks of the school year, saving teaching time earlier on (much of which is now used for C.S.E. examinations in the period from Easter to Whitsun) and releasing students as soon as they have finished their exams. Prospective sixth formers could return for induction courses at the end of the examination season, which ought to be much shorter than at present. Much of this is already taking place in well organised schools; the assessment and certification of G.C.S.E. will be of higher quality, and become accepted more readily, if the necessary time is provided from the outset. Such decisions are best left to schools, local authorities, and the examining groups, who are on the spot and have a good grasp of what is both possible and desirable in the next decade.

Chapter Three

REFERENCES

(1) G.C.S.E. - General Criteria, p.2. DES publication, HMSO 1965.
(2) Ibid, p.2.
(3) Ibid, p.5.
(4) Ibid, p.9.
(5) G.C.S.E. - A General Introduction, p.9. DES publication HMSO 1985.
(6) Reference has been made to the subject criteria published by the DES in these three subjects, but comment has been introduced between the sections where considered appropriate.
(7) G.C.S.E. National Criteria - History. DES publication, HMSO 1985.
(8) G.C.S.E. National Criteria - C.D.T. DES publication, HMSO 1985.
(9) G.C.S.E. National Criteria - Mathematics. DES publication HMSO 1985.
(10) Ibid, p. 5 - 7.
(11) Criterian Reference Measurement - W.S. Popham Prentice Hole Inc. New Jersey, 1978.

Chapter Four

G.C.S.E.   INSIDE THE SCHOOL

There is a danger that the tremendous burden which schools will have to face in introducing the new examination system, could produce a situation where the pupils, for whose benefit most of the changes will be made, will not be sufficiently well informed, and are yet expected to understand the changes, without proper briefing. This must not happen. The main purpose of the reform is to benefit pupils in schools; all other considerations, whether they are the Secretary of State's ideas on the curriculum, the problems of examination boards in servicing schools, and the organisation of the school itself, must be subordinate to the needs of pupils. This requires careful planning and decisions, as to which pupils, at what stage, and in what manner, they need to be informed of what G.C.S.E. is all about. This exercise must be done thoroughly and on the basis of a careful plan, bearing in mind that the real experts in the whole business are secondary school teachers. Colleagues in primary or middle schools cannot be expected to acquire detailed information within the short time available for launching G.C.S.E., although they should certainly not be forgotten in the whole exercise. There is a paramount need to send suitable information and adequate briefing to primary school teachers, bearing in mind that the secondary examination system cannot be expected to occupy a high priority in their day to day teaching. Parents too, will have been accustomed to the dual system, and their attitudes will inevitably rub off on their children. Some suggestions for dealing with these issues are made in Chapter 7, but they need to be borne in mind in designing a proper briefing programme for the pupils inside the secondary school.

G.C.S.E. INSIDE THE SCHOOL

Schools will face a double task: first and most urgently, those youngsters already in secondary schools, and in the first four year groups, will require early information, since they will be working to the new syllabuses for the new examination from the autumn of 1986 onwards. At the same time, steps will need to be taken to ensure that all new entrants to the school and of course their parents, know about G.C.S.E., and as soon as possible forget all about G.C.E. 'O' level and C.S.E.

It is of tremendous importance that right from the start, pupils should look towards the new system as presenting them with opportunities which substantially improve their chances of a good performance compared with the examinations being discarded. Whatever the deficiencies of the dual system, whatever the growing pains which will no doubt be experienced, whatever individual reservations about syllabus content and assessment procedures, the need is for a positive presentation to the school community. The considerable problems to be faced and solved should not protrude to such an extent that they confuse, and possibly disturb, the pupils. A unified secondary system requires a unified examination procedure, and this has been achieved. The first requirement is therefore, a clear statement that the new examination will be available to all (or nearly all) pupils, and that they can be expected to pass it. The old query: will I take G.C.E. or C.S.E.? What and who will decide which examination I take? should be replaced by stressing the unity of purpose and the single, final target for everyone in the school.

Having said that, more detailed explanations should be based on the following topics:-
1. Why G.C.S.E. has replaced 'O' level and C.S.E.
2. The advantages to be gained from the new system.
3. Subjects available in the school.
4. The grading scheme.
5. Who marks the papers, and the place of oral examining. If schools run mode 3 an additional explanation will need to be given here.
6. The timing of the examination in the school year, i.e. largely after Whitsun, as for G.C.E. This will need to be stressed particularly to pupils who might previously have been included in the C.S.E. target groups, and who have been accustomed to having the examination earlier, i.e. before Whitsun. Variations for oral and practical examinations should be stated.

7. Differentiated papers, differentiated questions, and continuous assessment schemes.
8. Names and basic information about the examination boards for which the school is entering its pupils. A statement as to when examination results will be available - most likely in August, as for G.C.E.
9. Fees payable. In most cases, these will be paid by the local authorities, but it is as well to state this and any variations which might arise with re-takes.
10. Relationship between current syllabuses in operation and new syllabuses being introduced.
11. References to teaching materials, especially textbooks and equipment.

Publicity material is already available from the examination boards and groups in addition to a leaflet already issued[1] by the Department of Education and Science. However, pupils and parents pay far more attention to authoritative statements which come from the school and it is therefore advisable for schools to produce appropriate statements, or perhaps a special newsletter for parents giving information of the kind mentioned above, either as substitute for, or in addition to, any material which is issued by external sources. Schools are far more likely than either the examination boards, the local authority or the D.E.S to find the right approach and the right method of communicating with their own pupils. The need is to provide adequate information at the right time, avoiding possible confusion through overloading on the one hand, or not providing enough information, on the other, due to the hectic nature of the school day. It is therefore a good idea to plan the method of dissemination of information over a period of time.

Information will need to be transmitted to pupils in various ways and by various people. A planned approach could be based on the following procedures operating inside the school:
1. Distribution of prepared material to forms by form teachers in a special form period, with a request, and time provided, that it should be read.
2. Briefing of various year groups.
3. Dissemination of information by subject teachers - i.e. subject briefings.
4. Availability of machinery to deal with individual queries, possibly through the school's examination officer.

G.C.S.E. INSIDE THE SCHOOL

Each procedure has its advantages and disadvantages. Form teachers are busy people and inundated with administrative tasks which get in the way of teaching. Whilst it may be assumed that some staff briefings will have taken place before pupils are approached, the nature of school life is such that one cannot expect the new tasks to be accommodated without some adjustment of the school's tiemtable. The need is for special and longer form periods than the twenty minutes in place of assemblies. The same applies to year meetings, many of which have to concern themselves with a multiplicity of business. At subject teacher level, the pressures of covering the syllabus are forever with the teachers, and again, special time needs to be put aside. The need is therefore for a phasing over a period of time which should not be so short as to lead to congestion caused by too much being communicated all at once, nor so extended that the impact is lost. Weekly sessions spread over half-a-term would probably suit most schools, and the following plan is suggested as a useful approach:

Week 1. Form meetings. Special form period (replacing an assembly, or year meeting or a teaching period) for an introductory explanation by form teacher and distribution of material.

Week 2. Year meetings. Explanation of how G.C.S.E. will affect the particular year group, with emphasis on dates and timetables.

Week 3. Subject briefings. These are important and at least a full teaching period per subject will need to be devoted to information and discussion. Ideally, this exercise should be co-ordinated carefully, and extend over a period of two or possibly three weeks. On the assumption that most pupils would take between six and nine subjects, a decision needs to be made as to which subjects, and how many, should be tackled in one week, and which in another. Four sessions per week will probably be the maximum which most schools will be able to permit themselves, bearing in mind other pressures and the need to spread the information. Ideally, syllabuses and question papers should be available for distribution. Depending on the year group, outline syllabuses will suffice in many cases.

The above is a basic programme to explain and involve the pupils in the launching of G.C.S.E., but two further additions will add to the quality of the exercise:

G.C.S.E. INSIDE THE SCHOOL

1. Working of mock papers. Whilst this should not, at this stage, be the kind of mock examination which many schools hold as part of their normal academic programme some months prior to the actual examination, a few sample papers will make an impact and increase the general sense of awareness of the change. Hopefully, specimen papers can be obtained from the examination boards, to reduce the workload on the school.
2. Marking. The marking of these papers on the basis of the new marking scheme, to be followed by discussion and feedback from pupils, can be a valuable exercise. Pupil involvement in the exercise - each others' papers being marked - can be stimulating, though proper briefing is needed.

Such a programme should ensure that pupils are reasonably well acquainted well before the introduction of the G.C.S.E. with the exception of those in the fourth years in 1986, who will have to start on the new syllabuses in September of that year and need to be treated with particular urgency. For them, a shortened and accelerated programme is needed, with subjects being selected on a sample basis. However, bearing in mind that the first examinations will not be held until 1988, the programme for other year groups could be taken at any time within the next twelve months, though there is a lot to be said for a fairly compact programme for the whole school.

The impact on extremely busy overworked and often stressed teachers in devising and implementing such a programme should not be underestimated. First and foremost, it requires the ready co-operation and goodwill of all members of staff, and this cannot in the present climate, be expected to be forthcoming, however well supported the introduction of G.C.S.E. as an educational reform may be, unless there is clear evidence to all teachers that local education authorities, examination boards and the school administration itself, show a keen sense of awareness of the need to create time. This time must be found within the school day, and if adequate briefing of schools staff are to be achieved, the best way is to make available a whole school week, providing a reasonable chance to reach all teachers. This means making available a concentrated period of time during which staff can devote themselves to getting the exercise off the ground without having to teach

G.C.S.E. INSIDE THE SCHOOL

as well. The local education authorities and the
D.E.S. should quickly agree to an additional week's
holiday for the pupils, during which schools staff
can get on with the job. It would be reasonable
for the local education authority to spell out a
basic programme, or alternatively, receive and
approve such programmes from the schools and their
governing bodies, to ensure that proper plans have
been drawn up. However, there is no doubt at all
that the gain in quality and subsequent performance
by putting aside a training week[2] for all secondary
schools would be immeasurable in terms of creating
goodwill, and an excellent investment in resource
management. Indeed, there is every likelihood that
without such a training week, the whole exercise
could be at risk. The present training plans aimed
largely at departmental heads, are totally
inadequate, the target group of teachers too
narrowly conceived, and the exercise too centralised
to penetrate the schools. The examination groups
have already costed the modest programme in training
and have made representations to the Secretary of
State, with little hope of the money being available.
The local authorities' associations have asked for
the postponement of the introduction of G.C.S.E.
for one year because the need for training is being
increasingly recognised. Central government needs
to understand and support a decentralised approach,
with the schools themselves seen as the senior
partners. The publication of manuals by the
Secondary Examinations Council [3] and by the Open
University, [4] will hopefully, provide some good
material, but the assumption that these manuals will
be read by teachers with the degree of attention
required, should not be made without careful
consideration of where the time is to come from.
Therefore, the provision of a training week,
containing the vital elements of a programme to be
discussed in the following pages is by far the best
way forward.

There are several other ways in which some time
may be found, hopefully, in addition to the training
week. First, the period following the present
public examinations which normally end in the last
week of June, or the first few days of July, and
when many fifth formers and certainly upper sixth
pupils are not in school, could be utilised for
further developmental work. Here again, it is
essential to understand that in very many schools
this period is already taken up with activities,
which cannot be accommodated in a crowded term

schedule, with induction courses for new pupils, particularly those who enter the sixth form, and with preparations for the start of the new school year in September. There is therefore, not a great deal of slack, but the possibility of utilising at least some days during the last two or three weeks of the 1986 summer term should be seriously considered. Indeed, schools are likely to be forced to carry out such a programme in a piecemeal fashion if G.C.S.E. is to start with even the most basic preparation by the autumn of 1986. If there is a postponement to 1987, the pressure would be reduced.

Another way of meeting the challenge is by the use of supply teachers. If no agreement can be secured between local education authorities, teachers' unions and the D.E.S., then local education authorities may decide to act individually in this matter. The provision of supply teachers to make possible a reasonable training programme in school time, should not be seen as an additional expense, but rather an investment in making the most productive use of such time. The extent to which such supply teachers are used will depend on whether or not a decision has been taken to allow a training week. Assuming that the basic training need for each teacher is to have the equivalent of five working days, then the staff of a secondary school of, say sixty teachers, would require the equivalent of 300 teaching days to accommodate the exercise. Clearly, the use of supply teachers would not be nearly as efficient as closing the schools for a week and allowing the co-ordinated programme of training described earlier. However, by targeting the supply teachers towards various departments, at different times it would be possible to accommodate at least part of the programme described earlier. If it is impossible to obtain a week for the training programme, then at least two-day closure, supplemented by supply staff, could be considered as an alternative, though again, would not nearly be as efficient as a week's closure.

In planning an in-service training programme for a school staff, decisions have to be made as to who needs to know what, when and the extent of detail required. The exercise will need to be conceived at various levels as follows:
1. A programme for all members of staff;
2. a programme for departmental heads in charge of subjects;
3. a programme for senior members of staff,

including heads, deputies, directors of studies, co-ordinators and examination officers.

These groups do of course, overlap, and in suggesting a division which reflects the most common staffing structures found in schools, the need for inter-communication should remain paramount. However the following matters will need to be known and discussed by all members of staff, and can thus form the basis of a suitable and compact training programme:

1. Syllabuses for G.C.S.E.:
   (i) Concepts
   (ii) Content
   (iii) Loading (i.e. amount of matter to be covered)
   (iv) Differentiation (in papers and questions)
   (v) Impact of national criteria
2. Target groups for G.C.S.E.:
   Differences and similarities with the old system
3. The grading scheme
4. Criteria referencing
5. The provision of modes 2 and 3 in the new system
6. Timetables
7. Communication and publicity
8. Resource implications
9. Outline of constitution of examination groups and freedom of choice.
10. The impact of G.C.S.E. on the whole school organisation.

Individual sessions devoted to each theme should be led by those colleagues who have already undergone sufficient training to speak with authority on at least some of the themes. If a training week is available, members and staffs of examination boards, local authorities advisors, Her Majesty's Inspectors, chairpersons and secretaries of advisory groups, and examiners, could implement such a programme with a high degree of competence. However, it is important to conceive the exercise as a problem solving one and not merely lecture sessions by outsiders who come into the schools telling teachers what to do. Each school must grapple with its own problems, and it is the teaching staffs of the schools who have the detailed knowledge which cannot come from outside. They will know the best ways of implementing the programme for their pupils, given a proper lead, and carefully devised framework. The need is not merely to provide information, but to enable discussions to take place involving all teachers. The structure of any conference should reflect this by allowing smaller discussion groups to raise specific issues which need clarification, as well as suggesting the best methods of implementation at school level by the whole staff, led by the head. Headteachers will clearly face a considerable professional task in gaining the overview necessary to lead their staffs.

The task is a demanding one for heads of secondary schools, most of whom are overworked, and in a stressful professional situation since the impact of industrial action both in 1984 and 1985. Whatever the outcome of the dispute between teachers and the employers, whatever the rights and wrongs claimed by various parties, the additional workload and stress on heads and deputies, and other senior personnel in schools should be clearly understood and appreciated by all parties concerned with G.C.S.E. Headteachers will need to be selective in the material they absorb, concentrate on the main pedagogic and organisational matters to be dealt with, leaving individual subject heads to lead their own departments, and ensure that feedback machinery is available from their own staffs to identify problems quickly and provide at least some solutions. The role of the head in G.C.S.E., should be seen as primus inter pares, leading a staff of professional teachers in order to advance the educational interests of the pupils. This will inevitably mean talking in plain language to resource providers, politicians and parents, a necessary skill heads should possess, with that degree of firmness one may expect from persons exercising a high degree of responsibility.

A training session for departmental heads, including the general themes already stated, will need to relate to individual subject areas, and the agendas for departmental meetings will need to be extended to accommodate the following themes:-
1. Agreement on a time scale followed by all subject teachers to accommodate the switch from the old system to the new, with those who have to take G.C.S.E. in 1988 being given clear priority.
2. Composition of teaching groups. This will take account of whatever degree of differentiation is to be accepted and considered acceptable.
3. Resource considerations. This is an important issue and is therefore, discussed separately, as it applies to all departments, but should figure on separate departmental agendas.
4. Syllabus revision. The need is not only to introduce the new syllabuses for years 4 and 5,

but to take a close look at the syllabus content for earlier years, to discuss to what extent any changes may be necessary to accommodate and prepare for the targets set by the new examination.
5. Choice of examination board/group. This will require detailed discussion, although the decision may well be taken elsewhere. Many schools use more than one examination board for the G.C.E., and all schools submitting candidates for both G.C.E. and C.S.E., have used at least two different sets of boards. The advantage as seen by departmental heads of having the freedom to choose a particular syllabus will need to be set against other considerations, and in particular, an evaluation of how far it will be possible to influence procedures and policies outside the region of the group is needed. There will be many advantages of staying within one group, a point for further discussion in Chapter 5.

Agendas for meeting of senior staffs - (heads, deputies, directors of studies, co-ordinators and examination officers) should be concerned with the following issues:
1. Strategy for implementation of G.C.S.E. - an overview of what needs to be done, when and how.
2. Staff development. Identification of issues for staff meetings, departmental and other meetings.
3. Provision of information - policy to be followed inside the school for
   (i) pupils
   (ii) staff
   (iii) publicity and communication for outside use, particularly aimed at
   (a) parents, (b) employers, (c) primary teachers, (d) other users (this point is discussed in more detail in Chapter 7).
4. Resource implications.
   This is a vital issue and requires detailed discussion of the following:
   (i) examination of existing resources
   (ii) costing of new books and materials required for introduction of syllabuses, following estimates provided by departments.
   (iii) costing of publicity material
   (iv) calculation of time required for implementation
   (v) planning of overall programme.

Details of costings are vital if the support of governors for additional resources is to be obtained, and pressure put on local education authorities to make available at least some of the additional resources required. Whilst the provision of new resources required can be phased, there is no doubt that they will be required. G.C.S.E. cannot be introduced by simply 're-tooling', using existing textbooks to 'make do'. In some cases, this will be possible, at least for a time, but the nature of the new examination system will require a vast development programme for new teaching materials and texts. However, there is also some real saving to be obtained by the introduction of the new system, particularly in terms of human resources, and when papers are presented to governors and local education authorities this needs to be spelled out very clearly. Teachers will save enormous administrative time which can also be costed separately.

5. Curriculum.
    (i) Consideration of common core subjects.
    (ii) The option system relating to G.C.S.E.

Schools will no doubt wish to review their policies in order to maintain a balanced curriculum through their option systems operating in Years 4 and 5. As the separation of G.C.E. and C.S.E. target groups will no longer be necessary, option systems should be much simpler to operate. Providing the proposals to institute distinction or merit certificates are dropped, there should be no problem in maintaining a balanced curriculum.

6. School organisation
    School policy with regard to
    (i) setting
    (ii) interest grouping
    (iii) mixed ability grouping.

It is in the structure of the option groups operating in nearly all secondary schools in the 14 - 16 age groups where the new system is likely to yield the greatest benefits in resource terms. Most syllabuses are designed in such a way as to allow considerable overlap. This means that the separate timetabling of G.C.E. and C.S.E. groups of varying and sometimes uneconomic, sizes, will no longer have to happen. Under the dual system, the different sized option groups which many schools maintain in order to provide a reasonable choice have always had to take account of two different examinations, especially in the many cases when G.C.E. 'O' level and C.S.E. syllabuses diverge. Under the new system, the principle of overlap combined with the common core approach will provide a real way forward. Setted groups can be geared to differentiated papers in any number of subjects where schools wish to operate sets. In other cases however, teachers will find it both more convenient and pedagogically more advantageous in accommodating teaching towards additional papers, which may be taken by some pupils, within the same teaching group. This should mean that the size of option groups will not show such variations as under the old system and will certainly be more economic. Clearly, the extent to which different group sizes can and will be organised depends on a variety of factors, not least the staffing levels of the school, the demand for various subjects, the availability of specialist teaching spaces, the need for many schools to maintain minority subjects, and a host of other considerations. Nevertheless, overall planning will be substantially eased, and the organisation of schools should become less complex once the common system is established.

7. Entry procedures.

The tremendous burden which schools are having to carry under the dual system is only too well known to those who have been faced with the separate entry forms and differing procedures required for the G.C.E. and the C.S.E. boards. However good the computerisation of entries, the programming and processing of thousands of individual subject entries begins in most schools immediately after Christmas, and takes up valuable time throughout the spring term. Apart from the mechanics of entering, the many individual discussions which take place between pupils, teachers and parents as to whether their subjects should be taken at G.C.E. or C.S.E. level, or for the 16+ papers, or as an insurance policy - both G.C.E. and C.S.E. - are enormous tasks which will either totally disappear or be considerably simplified. Clearly, discussions as to which papers individual pupils are to take will continue, but will be much more straightforward than the difficult decision, usually made at 14, as to which examination a candidate should take two years later.

Assuming that many schools will enter for the examining groups in their region, the whole entry procedure will be simplified. However, the following points are of particular relevance to examination officers:
1. The processing of entry forms
2. Entry costs
3. The possibility of dual entries for

differentiated papers, continuing the tradition of 'insurance policies' for borderline candidates.
4. Examination timetables, assuming that freedom of choice operates at departmental level.
5. Policy with regard to re-takes, deferred entries and early entries.
6. 'Top-ups' for pupils who seek to improve their grades in the sixth form, or earlier if the entry is made at the end of the fourth year.

The examination boards and the new groups which unite them, can be expected to reflect the requirements of schools, and there is already considerable evidence that the staff of the boards are sufficiently sensitive to take account of these. All examination groups need to be financially viable, and it is highly probable that their constitutions will carry forward the C.S.E. tradition of broadly based representation, including representation by local education authorities. This point is further explored in Chapter 5, but allowing for growing pains, present indications indicate a positive approach. The sooner and the more effectively schools make their requirements known to the examination boards, the more likely these boards are to respond positively to what is needed. The long controversy as to the extent to which examinations lead the curriculum or are curriculum led, will certainly not be eliminated. However, the emphasis is likely to shift towards the issue of national criteria as the main constraint on syllabus growth and development. Whatever the eventual outcome of the national criteria debate, it is for the schools themselves to state clearly what they expect from the new system, and to press for modification, simplification and flexibility as part of the bargain of pioneering a major educational reform.

Chapter Four

REFERENCES

(1) <u>G.C.S.E. - The New Examination System at 16+</u>.
A leaflet for parents published by the
Department of Education and Science, 1985.
(2) The provision of <u>time</u> is at least as important
as training; indeed, those teachers, mainly
departmental heads, for whom training is
envisaged, will need time to pass on the
benefits of their training to other colleagues.
This has been communicated to the Secretary
of State both by the examining groups in a
deputation to Sir Keith Joseph on 8th May 1985,
and again by a group representing the National
Union of Teachers at a meeting with him on
9th September 1985.
(3) The centrally conceived training programme by
the Secondary Examinations Council envisages
three major phases of training:
Phase 1: The preparation of manuals and videos to
support phases 2 and 3.
Phase 2: Seminars for 60,000 teachers (mainly
departmental heads) to be released for the
equivalent of 2 to $2\frac{1}{2}$ days from their duties.
Phase 3: The training of all teachers locally.
How the latter is to be achieved has not yet
been settled. However, the training programme,
whilst useful, does not go far enough, the need
to provide programmes for the whole teaching
staff of a school, along the lines suggested.
(4) The Open University has been commissioned by
the Secondary Examinations Council to publish
one manual for each subject, containing a set
of specific criteria, including guidance on the
issue of differentiation. The names will be
accompanied by videotapes of about 20 minutes
duration and it is intended that each teacher
receives both a manual and the video notes in

his/her subject.

Chapter Five

THE NEW EXAMINING GROUPS

The present examinations are administered by separate G.C.E. and C.S.E. boards in England, Wales and Northern Ireland. The G.C.E. boards are responsible for the conduct of all examinations leading to the General Certificate of Education at 'O' and 'A' level. These are the Joint Matriculation Board; the University of Cambridge Local Examinations Syndicate; the Oxford and Cambridge Schools Examination Board; the Southern Universities Joint Board for School Examinations; the University of London Schools Examination Board; the University of Oxford Delegacy of Local Examinations and the Associated Examining Board. The majority of the G.C.E. boards, as is evident from their titles, are directly connected with universities and derive their constitution, status, powers and functions from their parent universities. However, this is not the case with the Associated Examining Board, which is the newest of the G.C.E. boards, and was established particularly to promote new syllabuses and attract entrants from the growing further education sector in the post-war era. However, it has long since been firmly established in the schools, having taken early roots in technical and secondary modern schools.
   There are eleven C.S.E. Boards

   Associated Lancashire Schools Examination Board.
   Northern Regional Examination Board.
   North West Regional Examinations Board.
   Yorkshire & Humberside Regional Examinations
                                          Board.
   The East Midland Regional Examinations Board.
   The West Midland Examinations Board.
   The East Anglian Examinations Board.
   London Regional Examining Board

THE NEW EXAMINING GROUPS

Southern Regional Examinations Board
South-East Regional Examinations Board
South-West Examinations Board

These are regional bodies set up following the publication and acceptance by the government of the Beloe Report; they all administer examinations in well defined regions, which coincide with the areas of local education authorities. However, in Wales, the Welsh Joint Education Committee has, for a number of years, administered both the G.C.E. and C.S.E. examination, and in 1984 there was an amalgamation of G.C.E. and C.S.E. boards in Northern Ireland, so that in Wales and Northern Ireland both examinations, though separate, have already been administered by joint bodies even before the decision to have a common system of examining was announced.

Under the new examination system, the G.C.S.E. and C.S.E. boards are required to come together in examining groups, and in addition to Wales and Northern Ireland, four such groups have been constituted in England. They are the Northern Group, the Midland Group, the London and East Anglia Group and the Southern Group. The examination boards making up these groups are as follows:

Northern Group - G.C.E. board: Joint Matriculation Board.
C.S.E. boards: Associated Lancashire, North Regional, North-West Regional and Yorkshire and Humberside Regional Boards.

Midland Group - G.C.E. boards: University of Cambridge Local Examinations Syndicate, Oxford and Cambridge Schools Examinations Board, Southern Universities' Joint Board for Schools Examinations.
C.S.E. boards: East Midlands Regional Examinations Board, The West Midlands Examinations Board.

London & East Anglia Group - G.C.E. board: University of London School Examinations Board.
C.S.E. boards: East Anglian Examinations Board, London Regional Examining Board.

Southern Group - G.C.E. boards: University of Oxford Delegacy of Local Examinations, Associated Examining Board.
C.S.E. boards: Southern Regional Examinations Board, South East

81

THE NEW EXAMINING GROUPS

Regional Examinations Board,
South West Examinations Board.
A list of the boards in the new groups and addresses for enquiries appear in Appendix.

The examining boards for the G.C.E. and C.S.E. are different in origin, constitution, operation and philosophy. There are two major differences:

The G.C.E. boards are national bodies, accepting and attracting entries from schools and colleges all over the country, irrespective of geographical location. Several of them also have connections overseas and are thus bodies with an international reputation.

The C.S.E. boards are regional, and by virtue of their constitution, service closely defined geographical regions, with schools having to enter their candidates for the C.S.E. examination conducted by their regional board. Exceptions, mainly in the form of 'borrowed' papers, i.e. one board agreeing with another to allow its paper to be used, are few. The whole C.S.E. system was designed deliberately to maintain regional and local links between schools and examining boards.

The second difference is in the composition of the boards. The G.C.E. boards have a number of member interests, but in the majority of them the university interests predominate. The C.S.E. boards whilst allowing for minority interests, are largely composed of teachers and representatives of local education authorities. The teachers are nominated by the professional associations (and also by their l.e.a's) and teacher control of the C.S.E. boards has been their major constitutional feature. This was a specific recommendation when the Beloe Report was accepted by both teachers and the government. The philosophy of teacher control of C.S.E. reflected the educational mood of the early 'sixties. The teachers were to have the greatest possible freedom to develop curricula in the schools, reflecting the individual needs of schools and candidates. They were therefore the people who knew best what was required and were given the say in how the new examination, the C.S.E., should be conducted. The provision of three types of syllabuses, mode 1, designed and examined by the board; mode 2, designed by groups of schools and again examined by the board, and finally, mode 3, designed and examined by the schools themselves, reflected the philosophy of freedom in curricula design and the examining process which dominated the educational scene in the post-war era. The growth of mode 3 in particular, (it is estimated that some 4,000 mode 3 syllabuses are in existence) was in direct and deliberate contrast to the tightly controlled G.C.E. syllabuses, although in the course of time mode 3 became available under G.C.E. also, but only forming a small element of G.C.E. entries. However, it would be wrong to assume that the G.C.E. boards are without teacher influence. Their vital examinations committees and other sub-structures contain large numbers of heads and class teachers, and their subject panels frequently - especially in the case of London University - contain teachers nominated by the professional associations. However, their councils and governing bodies do not reflect this teacher influence and are a carefully balanced amalgamation of various interests, with the higher education sector often predominating. In the case of C.S.E. boards, control is firmly vested in the teachers, and in particular, the nominees of their professional associations, although for subject panels, teachers are usually nominated by local advisory groups. Although the local education authorities are in the minority on the governing councils, they control the Finance and General Purposes Committees of the C.S.E. boards and as such reflect the powerful influence of the l.e.a's, both in financial and educational matters. Such influence is less evident in the case of the G.C.E. boards.

The new examining system requires the different examination boards to function as groups. Whilst maintaining the separate identity of the boards, there is a clear expectation that they should function as corporate bodies without necessarily being constituted as such. The details of organisation, administration and the methods of co-operation are left to the groups themselves, who are required to draw up constitutions. The general criteria published by the Secretary of State simply states that the G.C.S.E. certificates are to be awarded by examining groups and not by individual boards, and that these certificates should include the names of the boards which comprise the group. There is a specific requirement that the different boards need to explain on the certificate their respective responsibilities for the standards of particular grades, the higher grades, A, B and C being the responsibility of the G.C.E. boards, and the remaining grades D, E, F and G that of the C.S.E. boards. There are further requirements that the

THE NEW EXAMINING GROUPS

examining groups need to reach agreement with the Secondary Examinations Council and the Department of Education and Science on a common form of certificate, that such a certificate will be countersigned by the Secretary of State for Education and Science (and by the Secretary of State for Wales in the case of Wales) and that an appeals system, whereby centres may, on behalf of their candidates, appeal against results awarded or against disqualifications, should be instituted. The principle of freedom of choice is firmly enshrined in the new examination and is in contrast to the regional procedures followed by the C.S.E. boards: the new procedures specifically state that examining groups may accept entries from schools throughout England and Wales.

The maintenance of separate examining boards within the new group system reflects both a recognition of the firmly established place of both types of examining boards in the educational world, and the need for compromise to get the system off the ground. Administratively, it would clearly have been tidier, more logical and more easily understood, if the present sets of boards had been swept away and new ones established to service the new system. However, such a radical approach was unthinkable. The G.C.E. boards occupy a powerful and strategic position in the examination world. Historically, they are the custodians of an academic tradition which still pervades the educational system of this country and the conduct of any public examinations without them is unacceptable. Furthermore, several of them are protected by Royal Charter[1] and it is doubtful whether any Secretary of State has the power to do away with them without going through a lengthy and complicated legislative process which would undoubtedly be challenged. In spite of the great expansion in the number of candidates offering themselves for the G.C.E. examination, G.C.E. syllabuses and papers are still for the majority of abler pupils. The remainder, in spite of the overlap between C.S.E. 1 and Grades A, B and C of G.C.E. 'O' level, are serviced by the C.S.E. boards who have the expertise to deal with the vast numbers of such candidates, as well as reflecting the powerful interests of both the teaching profession and the local education authorities. Attempts to override and sweep away such a powerful educational alliance would have met with such hostility and opposition that the new system would have been doomed from the start. The essential compromise reflected in the establishment of five groups of examining boards being constituted through the existing machinery, was an inevitable, but possibly an interim, solution. An examination of the development and possible functioning of the groups must therefore be seen in the light of what may well be a temporary position.

In attempting to create a new group identity whilst maintaining the separate existence of each board, the examining bodies have shown some variation in their approach. Two distinct models are emerging: one shows a strong move towards a unitary system and the other introduces the philosophy and features of federalism. The models overlap and are not necessarily opposed to one another, but nevertheless show distinct features.

What may broadly be called the centralist model is seen in the proposed arrangement for the Southern Examining group. The group sets itself the following objectives:
"Any administrative structure for the Southern Examining Group should meet the following objectives:
(i) The Group must provide an efficient educational and administrative service to centres, both in and out of the territory of the Group.
(ii) The structure should be cost-effective, taking into account the size and location of existing resources.
(iii) The structure must allow for effective participation by teachers and L.E.A's in the work of the Group.
(iv) Centres' present loyalties to boards must be retained and transferred to the Group.
(v) There must be satisfactory arrangements for the present staff of the five boards."[2]

In moving towards the achievement of these objectives, the Southern Group states specifically that some of its functions will be performed more efficiently if centralised, and there is a recommendation that a central administration office should be established, linked to a number of local offices. The functions to be formed by the central administrative offices are listed:

Central Administrative Office:
It is recommended that the central administration office shall undertake the following functions:
(i) Receives and processes entries and results, and deals with all queries relating to same.

(ii) Organises all despatches to centres, including syllabuses and regulations, entry forms, all other procedural documents, stationery, details of markers, question papers, etc., and answers all queries on same.
(IIi) Collates Group publications for print and despatch to centres, e.g., examination reports, Group circulars, examination statistics.
(iv) Liaises with local offices on all relevant matters and transfers such data as required.
(v) Maintains register of centres.
(vi) Undertakes in-house printing of Group documents (e.g. information sheets) as required
(vii) Stocks and sells Group publications.
(viii) Prepares examination timetables.
(ix) Arranges printing of syllabuses.
(x) Co-ordinates computer facilities of the Group.
(xi) Co-ordinates Group finances, and receives entry fees from L.E.A's/centres.
(xii) Prepares and co-ordinates Group regulations and examination procedures.
(xiii) Houses Group archives. [3]

However, even within this strongly conceived central apparatus, there is emphasis on the establishment of local offices and their functions are carefully defined, with particular sensitivity to maintaining contacts both with school centres and local education authorities: the local officers are detailed to undertake the following functions:

It is recommended that the local offices shall undertake the following functions:
(i) Undertakes servicing of those mode 1 subjects allocated to it by the Group, i.e. servicing of Group Subject Working Party, paper setting, revising and printing; appointment and training of markers and moderators; co-ordination of marking; administration of award procedure.
(ii) Answers all queries from its centres concerning syllabuses, assessment methods, etc. for all Modes 1, 2 and 3 examinations.
(iii) Organises course work arrangements.
(iv) Receives and processes modes 2 and 3 submissions.
(v) Builds and maintains contacts with centres and L.E.A's to provide advice and assistance as required, both on a general and on a subject specific basis. [4]

In addition, it is envisaged that the local officers may undertake certain data processing and financial functions in co-operation with the central administration.

The group also envisages the appointment of a chief executive officer, employed direct by it, together with a group secretariat. The local offices are situated in strategic centres, as indicated in the enclosed diagram.

Relationship between the Group Secretariat, the Central Administration Office and the Local Offices.

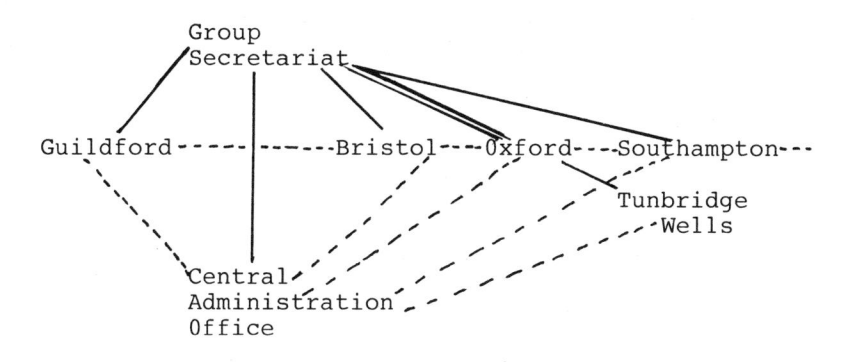

```
              Group
             Secretariat
Guildford---------Bristol----Oxford----Southampton---
                                        Tunbridge
                                         -Wells
            Central
            Administration
            Office
```

(Local Office for F.E. and out-of-Region centres).

(Four Local Offices for within-Region Secondary Centre).

———————————— = Control

------------- = Liaison

THE NEW EXAMINING GROUPS

The emergence of the Southern Group model links the concept of a unitary approach with the devolution of some responsibility to local groups and also recognises the historical role of the G.C.E. boards. In considering the location of the central administrative office, which is to be sited at Guildford, the headquarters of the Associated Examining Board, there is reference 'the historical willingness of the A.E.B' to host these arrangements. Again, in deciding where the group secretariat should be sited, Oxford is chosen, and again the 'historical willingness of the Oxford delegacy is specifically mentioned. The group secretariat is intended to service the major group committees, implement their decisions, co-ordinate the activities of the central and the local offices and generally help the major group committees in the development of policy. The group estimates that approximately twenty-five per cent of its subject entries come from out of region centres and is clearly anxious to maintain these entries in order to ensure the viability of the group. Therefore, one office is specifically charged with the responsibility of dealing with out of region entries. The proposed arrangement is sensitive and skilfully designed and has already drawn favourable comment among teachers and l.e.a's.

The London and East Anglian Group is adopting a somewhat different approach. The emphasis here has been to develop common procedures, but to leave much of the detailed work to the individual boards and avoid what the three boards concerned see as considerable expense, the setting up of a centralised office. Instead, a co-ordinating officer has been appointed with functions specifically designed to ensure that the overworked secretaries of the three boards are helped, and the administrative procedures of the three partners coincide as far as possible. Considerable progress has been made in the drafting of a constitution which sees the setting up of a council of some forty-five members to oversee the group activities as the main organ. This council is to consist of some thirty-five persons with equal representations for both the G.C.E. and the C.S.E. interests, with provision for the representation of higher and further education interests, employers, and other co-opted persons. The council is to be served by a small co-ordinating committee consisting of the Chairpersons and senior members of all three boards and the three secretaries. The co-ordinating body is seen as working out the details, for council, of major policy decisions to be taken without establishing an elaborate structure. There is to be a joint finance sub-committee, consisting of equal representations from the three boards, but answerable to the boards themselves rather than the council. The detailed work relating to the control of syllabuses, syllabus development and allied matters, are left with the subject panels drawn from the three boards, with co-operative and co-ordinating procedures as required.

The London Group also sees the continuation of its three centres at Colchester, where the East Anglian Board is housed, at London University, Stewart House, the newly built centre of the London University Examining Board, and at Wandsworth, where the London Regional Board is situated. The Group is particularly concerned with the need to ensure that training receives major attention, and has appointed a training officer. Whilst details of the various arrangements, including the important financial matters remain to be worked out, the development of this group, in which the writer has had a part, has proceeded well, eased by the fact that only three boards are involved. There is also particular sensitivity to the need to maintain the links which both the G.C.E. and C.S.E. boards have with their particular schools, and the local education authorities in their area. A great deal of detailed work remains to be done, and problems of different practices and administration to be sorted out. Bearing in mind the large number of candidates with varying ethnic backgrounds, particular sensitivity has been shown by the University of London Board in publishing a draft [5] on examination procedures which deal with sexism, discrimination and gender biases in G.C.E. examinations. This document faces squarely the criticisms which, it states, have sometimes been made with regard to the examination system. For example, it specifically identifies calls which have been made to re-write syllabuses, to highlight contributions made by females to history, art, music and English literature. The document also considers the evidence showing that females do not appear to be doing as well as males in the introduction of multi-choice tests, and makes recommendations in this respect. In a most interesting and significant conclusion the University of London Examinations Board states its policy as follows:-

"The following procedures for the detection and

removal of sexism and gender biases from the Board's examination papers were agreed.
Sexism
(a) The Board's existing moderation procedures for examination papers should be extended to include a 'sensitivity review' aimed at detecting sexist material.
(b) A small group of staff and experienced examiners should be set up to make a post examination review of all question papers issued, in order to detect possible examples of sexism. All such examples found should be referred to the appropriate Chief Examiners for comment.
(c) When examples of sexism are found they should be recorded and used in future training schemes together with possible non-sexist alternatives.
(d) When new or revised syllabuses are developed, the views should be sought of groups known to be actively researching into gender differences in responses to the particular subject.
Gender Biases
(e) All multiple choice questions and a selection of written paper questions should be monitored for gender differences in responses. Where educationally significant differences in response are noted, the results should be fed back to the Chief Examiner and possibly the Centres."[6]

The approach towards careful co-ordination of procedures of the three boards covers every aspect of examining. A careful timetable of events, including all aspects of the examination, and in particular, such vital matters as borderline review, procedures at standardisation meetings, the review of handicapped candidates, the interchange of scripts and the arrangement of co-ordination meetings between examiners and team leaders tied to a time scale, are meticulously stated. The co-ordination between the key people involved in the examining process have been worked out with particular care. Thus, the sample scripts from a centre to be despatched by assistant examiners, must be dealt with within forty-eight hours of the co-ordination meeting, and then sent to the Chief Examiner, whose comments must be communicated to the assistant examiner within twenty-four hours, including if necessary, requests for a further batch for monitoring before final marking begins. At the halfway stage, a further sample of scripts from each assistant examiner are checked by a chief examiner or team leader. If there is more than one examiner or team leader, they too, exchange scripts during the co-ordination procedure to ensure consistency of marking. A similar careful arrangement applies in considering borderline candidates, where the review includes candidates from schools whose results are markedly out of line with previous years, candidates who show considerable discrepancy of results in two or more papers, scripts where, despite the standardising and co-ordinating procedure, doubts remain about the marking and special consideration of candidates whose total subject marks places them within a specified range of marks below the grade boundary for the subject. Further procedures deal with partially absent candidates and there is also a procedure for special consideration cases for candidates whose work is thought to have been affected by physical disability, illness, accident, bereavement or other adverse circumstances occurring either before or during the examination. These procedures already apply to the joint 'O' level/C.S.E. examination by the London and East Anglian boards, and will certainly be carried forward when G.C.S.E. is off the ground.

The special provisions for handicapped candidates includes the allowance of extra time up to a maximum of twenty-five per cent for written papers, the provision of short, supervised rest periods, the possibility to take examinations in hospital or at home, the making of special arrangements where the handwriting of a handicapped candidate is difficult to read, the provision of braille or large print papers for blind or partially sighted candidates, and special arrangements for spastic or paraplegic candidates who can use typewriters, microwriters or other machines. Some of these provisions do, of course, exist already in the separate systems of G.C.E./C.S.E. examinations. Nevertheless, the impression which emerges from the careful review of procedures suggests that sensitivity and quality in the examining process are of paramount consideration in designing the new system. In spite of the enormous pressures caused by the introduction of national criteria, the need to get new administrative procedures off the ground, to deal with complex financial matters, the individual needs of candidates have been carefully preserved. Examining Boards are sometimes accused

THE NEW EXAMINING GROUPS

of having a responsibility to nobody but themselves, of being inflexible, and bureaucratic. A perusal of steps being taken, both to ensure a high standard of marking and the provision of special procedures, would suggest that the opposite is the case. It may well be that the quality of the examining process has not been adequately publicised or has simply not been communicated to the various parties, but there is little doubt that the quality is there.

Clearly, there is always the possibility of human error. Teachers with experience of examining over a long period, can point to unexpected and sometimes bizzare results. On the other hand, it is fair to point out that these are the exception rather than the rule. What is clear that in designing the new system, the examining boards are showing particular care to get the procedures right to ensure that the new system operates as fairly as possible, and that high professional standards in marking and moderating are being maintained and improved. There is also evidence of great sensitivity towards minority interests and special cases. It may well be, that at a time of falling rolls and the possibility of shrinking entries, the need to attract and maintain candidates is more clearly recognised than in the past. There is also the opportunity which the new system brings in overhauling procedures which may be well established, but have become set and perhaps sometimes appear inflexible. The need as well as the opportunity to evaluate and re-assess what is being done, the comparison between G.C.E. and C.S.E. boards, between procedures adopted by both sets of boards, coupled with the fact that the new system is to operate with a much higher degree of accountability than has been the case in the past, seems to have brought out the best in the examining process. This is not to say that all deficiencies have been obliterated. However, in the powerful moves being made towards forms of assessment other than by public examinations, it is pertinent to ask why a system based very largely on external mechanisms continues to survive. The fact is that the people who run the show, the examining boards, have a reputation for credibility and reliability. The existence of a complex apparatus bringing together professionals from schools, colleges, universities and the local authorities, who, by virtue of their constitutions, need to supervise their own operations with considerable care, is a feature of the educational system which should neither be taken for granted, nor accept too easily the criticisms and the denigrations to which it is sometimes subjected from those not directly involved. Examinations are for pupils who are adolescents, not theorists and philosophers. Adolescents have a strong sense of fair play and the general fairness of the public examination system is seen by them as one of its major assets. By and large, pupils in schools rise to the challenge of examinations, even like them, and accept what they try to achieve.

This attitude is also reflected in opinions of parents. They may not always be pleased with the results which their offsprings obtain, but it is seldom that one hears criticism that the system is totally unfair or not reliable. The users, too, whilst conscious of shortcomings of procedures which seek to give a picture of attainment gained over a long period of education, through examinations lasting only a few hours, nevertheless place considerable reliance on it. Employers and further and higher education interests, largely accept and very seldom challenge, the accuracy of examination grades obtained by candidates. The way different user interests interpret results varies tremendously; nevertheless, the framework of public examinations is conceived as being sound, with strong support for its continuation. The reform of the dual system was long overdue; but voices being raised in favour of a more radical reform, whilst sometimes strident, are few and far between. This may reflect ingrained traditional attitudes when set against the assessment and monitoring procedures emerging from such ventures as the new technical and vocational educational initiative. (TVEI). Here, the emphasis on testing skills and making judgments about tasks forming part of an educational design, is sometimes presented as a better and more attractive alternative to the more conventional system being discussed. However, TVEI, its policies practices and procedures, have to prove themselves. The outcome of the educational process cannot be judged on the basis of short term experiments, whatever claims are made in their favour. Such experiments must have a place in the dynamics of a changing educational world, but will themselves need to be subjected not only to vigorous examination by the professionals, but to the much more lasting and long term test, whether the outcome is acceptable to the users of the system

THE NEW EXAMINING GROUPS

It is a test, which, for many years the public examinations system has passed, in spite of problems and criticisms. This is perhaps because the rate at which the examination system changes, approximates to the rate of organisational and curricular changes in schools. This close relationship between schools and examining bodies, reflected particularly in the regional character of the C.S.E. examinations, seems to meet a need which is still felt at the present time, and which the present reforms are likely to meet.

The Northern Examining Association consists of the Joint Matriculation Board as the G.C.E. partner, the four C.S.E. regional boards, and its proposed constitution provide for representatives in equal numbers alongside other interests. The provisional arrangements for the membership of the N.E.A. councils are as follows: [7]

(a) Five representatives from each C.S.E. Board = 20
Twenty representatives from the J.M.B. = 20
Two representatives from each of the three Northern Local Education Authority Associations, = 6
Universities and/or polytechnics, the C.B.I. and the T.U.C. = 6

(b) One representative from each of the following Teachers' Unions:-
Assistant Masters/Mistresses Association
National Union of Teachers
National Association of Schoolmasters/Women Teachers
National Association of Teachers in Further and Higher Education
National Association of Headteachers
Secondary Heads Association = 6

Total 58

Here the main representation on the governing council is clearly through the boards, with special provision for the teachers' unions, which is likely to prove controversial, bearing in mind the different size of such unions and the Burnham principle, whereby the largest union, the N.U.T., had most representatives. However, it is likely that some of the representatives from the C.S.E. board will themselves be nominees of the teachers' association, so that representation of their interests may be achieved via the C.S.E. boards. There is then a finance advisory group, a much smaller body, containing two members from each of the C.S.E. boards, four members from the J.M.B., the chairman of the N.E.A. council and of the new N.E.A. examination committee, making a total of 14. The interesting point about this arrangement, which approximates that of the co-ordinating committee of the London Group is, that there seems to have been no objection to a majority for the C.S.E. interest. However, there is a clause which states that the G.C.E. and C.S.E. representatives respectively are regarded as equal partners, and that approval of formal proposals requires the agreement of both partners. The finance committees will be charged with implementing a common scale of fees, both for candidates and for examiners, and to consider other issues relating to finance and the attendant staffing matters.

The N.E.A. examinations committee however, returns to the principle of equal representation of both the G.C.E. and C.S.E. interests. Four representatives from each C.S.E. board giving a total of 16, are partnered by 16 representatives from the Joint Matriculation Board, half of whom are required to be serving teachers from N.E.A. centres, and two chairpersons. The functions of that committee are to determine the general principles of examination policy and procedures, and to deal with all matters relating to board based, i.e. mode 1, syllabuses, the arrangements for the award of grades, the monitoring and maintenance of comparability of standards within the N.E.A. group, and also in relation to other groups, and many other detailed matters. There is a specific requirement that the examination committee should make efficient use of 'existing human, financial and physical resources of the constituent board'. A rule that the J.M.B. should be responsible for the arrangements for the award of grades A, B and C and the C.S.E. boards for the awards of D, E, F and G, is contained in the draft constitution and reflects the national pattern. The N.E.A. also proposes to establish subject committees, where again the C.S.E. boards collectively provide eight persons, who are partnered by eight from the J.M.B., thus maintaining the principle of equality of representation of interests.

In considering the working of the arrangements, there is the interesting statement that the separate boards would continue to have what is termed 'a separate constitutional existence', but that they will have to merge their separate identities in order to combine the examining activities and

THE NEW EXAMINING GROUPS

functions to provide a single examining service'. There is a further statement that the C.S.E. boards will additionally have to merge their own separate identities to form a C.S.E. side. Some functions to be carried out by the boards are then defined, and deal mainly with the administration of centrally provided, board based syllabuses and the relevant procedures, except in the case of mode 3, where the boards will act as the regional agents of the examining authority. It would appear that the model here is similar to that of the Southern group, with the emphasis on the unitary rather than the federal principle, though details remain to be worked out.

The negotiations preceeding the formal constitutional arrangements, the rationalisation of procedures and the organisational changes, are both sensitive and time consuming. However, there is a clear recognition on the part of both the G.C.E. and C.S.E. boards that the community of interests which they have in getting the new system off the ground, is greater than any differences between them. To some extent, the movement towards a unified approach has been hastened by the attitude of the Secretary of State, and the Department of Education and Science, in leaving no doubt in anyone's mind that it is government which intends to oversee and to some extent, actually control, the G.C.S.E. The political issues underlying such an approach are far reaching and are part of the changing relationship between central and local government. However, what concerns us here are not the possible conflicts which may arise out of a centralist approach, but the functioning of the system as part of a nationally conceived exercise in response to a movement which has its origin in the grass roots in the schools. It should not be forgotten that the advocacy of a common examination system has come from the schools, from the teachers, from the teachers' unions and therefore from those closest to the coal face. The Schools Council, in its role as an educational parliament, advocated a common 16+ system throughout the seventies; the teachers' associations, notably the N.U.T.[8] but in partnership with the other professional associations, adopted a similar stance, and the C.S.E. boards themselves, although facing a possible threat to their existence, were likewise in the vanguard of the advocacy of a common system.

After the dissolution of the Schools Council by Sir Keith Joseph, the Secondary Examinations Council with Sir Wilfred Cockcroft as the Chairman and Chief

THE NEW EXAMINING GROUPS

Executive, was established in 1982. Its specific function is to advise the Secretaries of State on how the school examinations and assessment system can best serve the needs of the education service. The Secondary Examinations Council has three major responsibilities with regard to G.C.S.E.
(i) To ensure that all G.C.S.E. examination syllabuses in all modes, and all assessment, moderation, grading and certification procedures comply with the national criteria.
(ii) To develop draft grade criteria for each major subject, such criteria to be approved by the Secretary of State.
(iii) To produce an in-service training programme for teachers involved with G.C.S.E.
The Council, which consists of representatives nominated by the Secretary of State, a radical break with the tradition of elected representatives of member interests, has set up nineteen G.C.E. subject committees and a steering committee dealing with in-service training. The subject committees have forty members, one member drawn from each of the five C.S.E. examining groups, five others selected from nominations made by the subject associations, the teachers' associations, the local education authorities' advisory service, from industry and commerce and the higher education sector, with another member drawn from the corresponding 18+ subject committee dealing with 'A' levels. There is an observer from Northern Ireland, an assessor from Her Majesty's Inspectorate, and an assessor from the Council itself. Most of the work of the subject committees consists of the scrutiny of mode 1 syllabuses produced by the examining groups to ensure that they comply with the national criteria. This vetting procedure consists basically of a check list of points which relate to the subject specific criteria, and the S.E.C. therefore carries out a clear monitoring function on behalf of the Secretary of State. However, the S.E.C., very wisely, has realised that it cannot use the same procedure in vetting the considerable number of mode 2 and mode 3 syllabuses, and this responsibility has therefore been devolved to the examining groups themselves, using a similar check list, with the national subject committees sampling the work of the groups in these areas. All committees have been appointed for three years, and their terms of reference are worth quoting in full to indicate very clearly the powerful functions exercised by the S.E.C. in

THE NEW EXAMINING GROUPS

respect of all syllabuses;
"(a) to convert in their curriculum area the national criteria and any grade-related criteria into operational tools for monitoring G.C.S.E. syllabuses and assessment and grading procedures;
(b) to receive syllabuses and major amendments as submitted by the G.C.S.E. examining groups and, after proper consultation with the group concerned, recommend approval or reconsideration using the processes developed under (a);
(c) with all approvals under (b) to recommend a first date for conducting a monitoring exercise (scrutiny) on the operational examination;
(d) to suggest a rolling programme of scrutinies to comply with the S.E.C's overall programme;
(e) to propose members to be considered for scrutiny teams;
(f) to receive scrutiny reports for discussion and appropriate recommendation before despatch to the board concerned;
(g) to receive regular reports from the examining groups concerning previous scrutinies;
(h) to ensure that assessment, grading and scrutiny procedures and the relevant 16+ national criteria and any grade-related criteria subsequently developed are under regular review;
(i) to consider$_9$any other matters referred by Council".

It will be readily understood that the examination boards, whether G.C.E. or C.S.E., have watched the evolution of this powerful body with mixed feelings. Whilst there has been an acceptance that there needs to be a national body to oversee the operation, which is after all, nothing new, the extent to which both the Secretary of State and the Department of Education and Science are seen as influencing and controlling the operation of the S.E.C., have not been well received. Indeed, occasionally one has detected signs of irritability on the part of the S.E.C. itself in dealing with the Department of Education and Science. Whatever the politics of the situation, the examining boards see themselves as carrying the major responsibility of administering the new system, and co-operated by forming the G.C.E. and C.S.E. Boards' Joint Council for the 16+ National Criteria which did most of the spade work to get that part of the exercise off the ground. The exercise was completed by February 1985, when the final version of an agreed document was sent to the Secondary Examinations Council. The extent to which the Secretary of State and the Department of Education and Science modified or influenced some of the national criteria in various subjects have already been discussed in an earlier chapter, but once that exercise had been completed, there was no need for the joint body to continue.

However, whilst the Joint Council for the National Criteria has come to an end, the examination boards have themselves established a new national body - the Joint Council for G.C.E. and C.S.E. Boards. This is a highly significant development. The membership of that body, which was only formed in May 1985, and has recently agreed a constitution,$_{10}$ consists of all examination boards, which are represented through their groups, each group having two votes to accommodate both the G.C.E and C.S.E. interest. This new general council is poised to become an influential and powerful body in the examination world, and it will be interesting to see how its relationship both with the S.E.C. and the D.E.S. develops. The title - The Joint Council for the G.C.S.E. - which has already been adopted, reflects the community of interests of the examination world, and is intended to consider and convey the collective view of the groups to national bodies such as the D.E.S. and the S.E.C. Each examining group is represented by up to six members, with Northern Ireland having two voting members. There is a statement that decisions wherever possible, should be reached by consensus, and the council is asked to 'consider and where desirable, develop a common approach to the issues of common concern to the groups'. A secretary has already been appointed to serve for a two year period, supported by an administrative officer and small clerical staff. The chairperson can be appointed either from within, or from outside, the examination fraternity. It is highly significant that each group has agreed to make a financial contribution, roughly in proportion to its subject entries (based on 0.6 pence per subject entry) to enable the council to find the £40,000 needed to get off the ground. This willingness on the part of the groups, and consequently the boards, to accept financial responsibility indicates perhaps more than anything else, the way the examining groups are responding to what they see as the challenge of central control. In the old and now disestablished Schools Council, there was a meeting point for all educational interests, since all the examining boards took their places alongside nominees from the teachers' associations, from the world of higher and further education, the local authorities, the employers and also the parents. What had been achieved was a broad educational consensus which, whilst often showing a healthy diversity of views, nevertheless, functioned as a recognised educational parliament. The substitution for this arrangement by a nominated council, directly responsible to the Secretary of State, has given rise to a development where the examining boards have organised themselves into an autonomous body. Since they will be conducting the whole business of examining on a day to day basis, the influence of the new body is likely to prove considerable. Such a development reflects the changing nature not only of the examinations system, but of the educational scene as such in the country. The drift is towards polarisation of governmental policies and those of schools, teachers and local authorities.

The organisation of examination boards in a Joint Council has its forerunner in the Standing Conference of C.S.E. Boards which has been in existence ever since the C.S.E. Boards originated in 1964. Each board is represented and the annual meeting of the C.S.E. boards, taking place in various parts of the country, with a host board accepting the responsibility for the arrangements, has been a major event in the educational calendar for a couple of decades. The Standing Conference provides an opportunity to review common problems, to compare examination performances across the country, and to formulate common policies. At their 1984 conference, the C.S.E. boards had the difficult task to decide whether or not to accept the principle of freedom of choice as practiced by the G.C.E. boards. Bearing in mind that all the boards are regional, and that freedom of choice implies the existence of a national system, it is to the credit of the C.S.E. boards that they upheld the traditional freedom of schools and teachers to select those examinations which suits them best. After considerable debate, the Standing Conference of C.S.E. boards voted by a majority of 11 votes to 2 in favour of the freedom of choice principle.

What criteria should determine the choice of an examining board by a school? It is a problem which has occupied teachers for many years, ever since the introduction of public examinations. Suitability of syllabuses, statistics of grades published by the G.C.E. boards and personal ties of school teachers with certain examining boards, have all played a

large part in what has sometimes been a difficult decision with regard to the selection of a particular G.C.E. board. In the case of C.S.E., there has of course, been no such problem, since entries have been through the regional board, and therefore governed by geography.
When deciding which boards to chose for G.C.S.E. teachers in schools are already having particular regard to the following considerations:
1. Suitability of syllabuses.
As the syllabuses from the various groups reach the schools, a careful evaluation of their quality, suitability and relevance to the needs of the pupils is under way. In many schools, old loyalties will prevail; in others, the new system will provide the opportunity for a change of board.
2. Sensitivity of examination boards to the needs of schools.
This manifests itself in a variety of ways, not least the ability of the groups to simplify entry procedures, which under the dual system, have been time-consuming and sometimes cumbersome. The more straightforward the completion of an entry form, the less the complications which schools have to face at a time when they are short of resources, the greater the attraction of a particular board or group.
3. Appeals system.
This is likely to prove an important factor, as there is a difference between the procedures followed by the G.C.E. boards and the C.S.E. boards. The former see an appeal against marks obtained by a candidate in a school as an exercise which has to be done a second time and paid for. Schools which are dissatisfied with their results can be accommodated either by a clerical re-check, or by a re-marking of scripts, and are expected to pay the appropriate fees. Sometimes results are adjusted, but schools are known to complain that more often than not the result remains the same. Whilst the C.S.E. boards have a similar procedure, they also provide appeals panels or committees, which provide the opportunity for personal appearances of school representatives at hearings. The appeals machinery provided by a group could be a vital element in deciding which board is chosen by a school. It is interesting to note that the Northern Examining Association already has firm

plans for establishing an appeals panel which goes beyond considering the customary written statement submitted by the head of a centre, and allows the appellant to appear and speak to the submission at a hearing. Whilst such a procedure can be time-consuming, it is nevertheless a vital component in establishing the new examination system, and ensures that there is a proper channel for the ventilation of grievances.

At the time of writing, the examining groups have not yet published their fees, but there has already been an expression of concern from the Secretary of State that these should not be increased. This is an unrealistic assumption. The developmental costs of the new system are such that it would not be unreasonable for the examining groups to ask for a substantial contribution from the government itself. No such contribution has been forthcoming, although the cost of investigating and developing the national criteria has to some extent been borne by the government. Since the groups are essentially in competition with one another, fee structures are likely to be a significant element in determining choice, though it has to be borne in mind that in the case of state schools, the fees are usually paid by the local education authority. But it is clearly impossible to develop the new system alongside the old without some developmental costs and at least a temporary increase of fees will therefore have to be expected.

Finally, in making a choice of examining board, teachers will be influenced by the opportunities provided for participating in shaping the new system. The teaching profession has been accustomed to direct and powerful involvement in the running of C.S.E. boards. Teachers have often chaired board meetings, occupied key positions on the major committees, and carried considerable responsibility for the entire developmental work of C.S.E. in the subject panels of their boards. In the G.C.E. boards, their influence may have been less pronounced at governmental level, but has been both effective and far reaching in committees and panels. Without the specialised knowledge, influence and support of the teaching profession, no examinations system can function. Furthermore, although professional tasks such as marking, examining and moderating undertaken by teachers are paid for on the basis of a complex fee structure, all systems rest on a tremendous amount of goodwill and the giving up of many hours of time in a voluntary capacity. At times of turbulence and industrial unrest in the schools, there is a risk that the new examination system may get off the ground rather less smoothly than many had hoped. There is particular concern that the time scale, with the first examination to be launched in 1988, requiring the new syllabuses to start in 1986, is too tight,[11] and that insufficient resources, either in terms of time or money, have been provided. Some teachers have said that it would be better to delay the start of the system for a whole year. The examining groups, whilst not favouring a postponement, have met the Secretary of State to explain in detail the need for investment in the necessary training required by many teachers to whom aspects of the examination will be new. The Secretaries of the boards have worked out detailed financial provision showing the developmental costs. So far, there has been no positive response on the part of the government to fund the new system to anything like the extent felt to be essential by those with the responsibility of running it. Although there is tremendous support throughout the world of education for the change, there are aspects of finance and resource management which casts some doubt that the starting date envisaged can be maintained. The Association of County Councils wants a postponement for one year, as does at least one major professional association, the N.U.T. However, mere postponement, without providing additional resources will not alter significantly the real challenge which is highlighted by the need for more time for teachers and others involved, and the need for more money to do things properly. The creation of a new examining system for the nation's schools is a major undertaking for all pupils, teachers, and examination boards, requiring the vision and commitment of the pioneer. This reform has been conceived, debated and finally achieved after more than a decade of experiment and compromise. The more money available, particularly in the early but vital stages, the better the new system will provide for the needs of the candidates.

Chapter Five

REFERENCES

(1) All English G.C.E. boards linked to universities may lay claim to a Royal Charter. The Associated Examining Board is a limited company, and the Welsh Joint Education Committee is bound by different rules. Some, but not all, C.S.E. boards are limited companies.
(2) Objectives published by Southern Examining Group, Guildford 1985.
(3) Ibid,
(4) Ibid.
(5) 'Sexism, Discrimination and Gender Bias in G.C.E. Examinations! University of London. London Schools Examination Board. 1985.
(6) Ibid.
(7) Constitutional Arrangements and General Principles for the Northern Examining Association.
(8) The N.U.T. has been a consistent advocate of a single examinations sytem at 16+, and its publications on the issue contains a wealth of information - see the following list:

'Examining at 16+' comment submitted by the National Union of Teachers. N.U.T. 1967.
'Examinations at 16+: proposals for the future: a policy statement. N.U.T., 1976.
Examinations at 16+: proposals for the future: N.U.T. 1976.
Discussion document on "Examinations at 16+: proposals for the future. N.U.T. 1976.
Examinations at 16+ and 17+: a conference sponsored by the N.U.T. (and held) at Hamilton House, 16 March 1977. N.U.T. 1977.
A guide to examinations: a paper presented to the N.U.T. Conference on Examinations at 16+

and 17+ (London) 16 March 1977, by D. Walker N.U.T. 1977.
Examining at 16+: the case for a common system N.U.T. 1978.
Examining at 16+: an N.U.T. policy statement. N.U.T. 1978.
Examining at 16 plus: an N.U.T. policy statement on proposals for a single system. N.U.T. 1980.
A single system of examining at 16+: national criteria. N.U.T. 1981.
Curriculum and examinations: memorandum of evidence submitted by the National Union of Teachers to the Education, Science and Arts Committee on Curriculum and Examinations for the 14 - 16 age group. N.U.T. 1981.
Examining at sixteen plus: a policy statement by National Union of Teachers. N.U.T. 1983.
A single system of examination at 16+: key educational issues. N.U.T. 1984.
All publications can be obtained from the N.U.T Hamilton House, Mabledon Place, LONDON WC1H 9BD

(9) Function relating to G.C.S.E. All terms of references of subject Committees.
Secondary Schools Examinations Council - 1984.

(10) Constitution and Financial Arrangements - the Joint Council for G.C.S.E. Agreed at London meeting of GCE and CSE boards, 18 September 1985.
The Council's Secretary is M. B. Swift.
Norfolk House, Smallbrook Queensway, Birmingham B5 4NJ.

(11) Peter Weston's excellent article 'Countdown to the G.C.S.E.' Times Educational Supplement 5 July 1985.

Chapter Six

G.C.S.E. - THROUGH STUDENTS' EYES

It is interesting and perhaps significant that the literature relating to public examinations contains practically no examples of what the pupils who take the examinations think of it all. The discussions relating to the present reform are no exception. A perusal of minutes of meetings, letters to the press, procedures at teachers' conferences, policy statements, whether they eminate from central government, local authorities, the teachers' organisations, or research bodies, contain very few, if any, references to the pupils' point of view. To some extent such attitudes reveal a survival of the assumption that pupils continue to be passive recipients of the educational process, although this is in direct contrast to modern pedagogy, which usually advocates a high degree of pupil participation in the learning process. When discussing this with colleagues and others involved in examinations, it became clear that there is considerable support for the notion of having some idea of what pupils think. Whilst some teachers express the view that pupils' opinions in a new situation not yet widely known could only be of limited value, the prevailing attitudes favoured an approach to pupils, not only on the specific issue of 16+, but on the whole business of examinations. In this chapter an attempt is made to let the pupils speak for themselves. In setting up a modestly conceived but highly interesting exercise, and discussing how it might be tackled with a small, but representative body of pupils covering the age range 12 - 19, the following features emerged:
1. Students, irrespective of ability, age group, background and sex, welcomed the opportunity of being consulted.
2. This welcome extended to handing in written

contributions, some of which were of considerable length, which were usually done in addition to the normal school work.
3. There was an almost complete acceptance of the need for an examination system as such, although the existence of a small, but articulate minority, who questioned that need also emerged.

The survey on pupils' attitudes was based on six questionnaires, drafted after consultation with the pupils themselves. These questionnaires were made available throughout the age groups, but with an invitation to different year groups to concentrate on one particular aspect. Only the minimum of explanation was given, so that the answers to the questions also revealed the existing state of knowledge, or lack of it, about the proposed change. Anonymous replies were accepted, pupils being told specifically that they had a choice whether or not they revealed their identities.

It is fair to state that the exercise was based on one school only, a large comprehensive school in East Anglia.[1] However, light sampling in a few other schools revealed that replies and attitudes were not significantly different. The school selected is not an area school, but draws its pupils from a wide catchment area, which at least makes it possible to test the assumption that what has emerged is likely to be fairly typical of attitudes of secondary school pupils towards the examination system. More sophisticated and carefully designed research projects might well reveal more refined results. The findings in this chapter must therefore take account of the limited nature of the exercise. Nevertheless, they yield valuable information on pupils' attitudes, and thus make it possible to consider such attitudes before implementing the new system. No attempt is made to draw definite conclusions, but extensive use is made of material produced by the pupils themselves, so that readers may form their own judgment.

The exercise involved new entrants to a secondary school whose admission age is 12, so that year 2 covers the 12 - 13 age group, year 3 aged 13-14; year 4 aged 14 - 15; and year 5 15 - 16; with both lower and upper sixth students being classified as the over sixteens, with a predominance of replies from the lower sixth. There was no significant difference in the replies from girls and boys, so that no sex differentiation was analysed.

G.C.S.E. - THROUGH STUDENTS' EYES

TABLE 1.
DETAILS OF QUESTIONS AND STATEMENTS
ON WHICH PUPILS WERE ASKED TO COMMENT.

YEAR 2:
In four years' time, you will be taking the G.C.S.E. (General Certificate of Secondary Education) examination in several subjects.
What are your feelings about examinations? Talk about your expectations, hopes, and if any, anxieties.

YEAR 3:
In 1986, you will start work on new syllabuses for a new examination, called G.C.S.E. (General Certificate of Secondary Education) which combines G.C.E. and C.S.E. in one examination system.
What do you think about this change, and what do you feel about examinations generally?

YEAR 3:
The grades in the present exam system are as follows:-

G.C.E.	C.S.E.
A	1
B	2
C	3
D	4
E	5
UG	UG

There are five pass grades. The new system (G.C.S.E.) will have seven grades as follows:

A
B
C
D
E
F
G
UG

F is the average grade.
What do you think of this change?

G.C.S.E. - THROUGH STUDENTS' EYES.

YEAR 4:
The present exam system, (both G.C.E. and C.S.E.) means that you normally sit exam papers subject to a time limit (usually $1\frac{1}{2}$ - $2\frac{1}{2}$ hours) at the end of the fifth year. The new exam, called G.C.S.E., (General Certificate of Secondary Education) will rely much more on

(i) Continuous assessment - work done during your fourth and fifth years;
(ii) Oral exams.
Give your opinion of this change.

YEAR 5:
Examinations are
(i) A useful way of assessing what you have learnt;
(ii) A necessary evil;
(iii) Unnecessary, and should be abolished in place of...
Consider these three statements and give your opinion.

YEAR 6:
At present, two separate examinations, the G.C.E. 'O' level (General Certificate of Education) and the C.S.E. (Certificate of Secondary Education) are taken, usually at the end of the Fifth year. From 1988 onwards, there will only be one examination - the G.C.S.E. (General Certificate of Secondary Education), instead of two. (The new syllabus for G.C.S.E., will start in the Autumn of 1986).
State your opinion of the proposed change.
If you have already taken either G.C.E. or C.S.E or both, relate your opinion to your experience of taking these examinations.
NOTE: Two statements were given to pupils in Year 3, since oral discussion revealed that there was particular concern about the grading system prior to allocation in G.C.E./C.S.E. groups.

TABLE 2 - ANALYSIS OF STUDENTS' REPLIES:
Of the 139 replies, 98 students put their names on the paper, and 41 sent in an anonymous reply:

Age Group	Number
12 - 13	27
13 - 14	25
14 - 15	24
15 - 16	25
Over 16	38
Total	139

G.C.S.E. - THROUGH STUDENTS' EYES.

When all the questionnaires had been received, an analysis was made of the points which occurred most frequently in all answers, irrespective of age group. These are analysed in Table 3 as follows:
(a) Attitudes to change in the system;
(b) Factors in favour of the change;
(c) Factors against the change;
(d) Statements against all examinations.

TABLE 3 - ATTITUDES TO CHANGE IN THE SYSTEM:

Need for better opportunities to achieve success
    More equality of opportunity
    Less confusing and more logical
    Better atmosphere within school community
    Better relations between students now taking G.C.E. and those taking C.S.E.
    Worries about change, and about examinations generally.
    Influence of results achieved by sisters and brothers.

Factors in favour of the change	Factors against change
Single target for all	Wide range of candidates to be catered for
A fairer system than the present one	Worry of not being stretched
Greater acceptability of G.C.S.E. compared with C.S.E.	Gap between G.C.S.E. and 'A' levels
Shorter examination season	Fear of being guinea pigs
Better marking methods	Fear that system will not get off the ground smoothly
Single grading system	
Continuous assessment	
More oral examining	Worry that existing qualifications will lose their currency
Fewer interruptions to school routine	
The hope that the time of the year at which exams are taken may be changed	Reservations about continuous assessment
	Concern at teacher judgment
A system in which everyone can succeed at something	More work to be done than at present
	Parents may prefer present system
Less divergence in results	Employers may prefer present system.

Against all examinations (small, but articulate minority) about 5%. These were their views:

110

G.C.S.E. - THROUGH STUDENTS' EYES.

Replacement by monthly or other tests (fairly popular)
Dislike of rigidity and unfairness of examinations
Preference for assessment by teachers
Worries that exams do not reveal true ability
However, the view that abolition of exams might be followed by something worse than exams was also expressed.

Perusal of the themes which featured most frequently in the pupils' answers correlates reasonably closely with matters which were felt to be of concern by teachers. However, what emerged strongly from the answers is the concern with the quality of the relationship between pupils having different examination targets. There is no doubt that there is considerable understanding, even among less articulate pupils, about the impact of a divisive and highly competitive examination system on a school community which strongly advocates harmony as a worthwhile goal in itself.

In the following text, extensive use is made of pupils contributions: they have been kept in their various age groups, and have been reproduced as submitted, with no corrections and no editing.

<u>Comments from second year pupils, age group 12 - 13</u>:

> I think that it is a better exam then haveing two different exams. It may sound silly but I am looking forward to my exams. I am a bit worried but I, am still looking forward. I think that it is good to have exams because it is good to see what you can do under stress.
>
> However it would be wonderful if we had no exams because under stress people tend to forget answers that they normaly know. If the work from your class years because in the class you do not worry and you can pick the best work from the year. Also a teacher before an exam can say 'I know that most years we have had this on the paper' You go home and revise what you teacher has told you and it doesn't come up on the paper!
>
> I don't really know much about the system but there is óne thing that I think about any exam is that they make me worry.
>
> Also I don't like being shut in a classroom either I think you should be aloud a break at some time.

G.C.S.E. - THROUGH STUDENTS' EYES

I only know a little about gcse I'm quite worried about the exam because I don't know if I'll pass but I want to pass.

The idea is good because if you are better at one subject and not so good at another you would still get high marks.

I think to new system showld by used but it sowd by beist on clasroom woork becouse people not feel well or mite get veri nerves and that cold ofect the result (remedial pupil)

I think the New system is the best because it gives everyone a chance to get a good mark because some you get 10 marks and some 15 which can get a good mark.

I know little about the system. I would be worried but not to much. it's a good to have the exam but not a very long one which last about 2 hours.

I know little about exams but I first thought I would be worried about approaching an exam. In a way I like the exam idea because it's a good test but I don't like the idea of being in a room for 2 hours or more on a hot day.

The new exams make it easier and better I think because you can pick your own questions and all the hard ones if you are cleaver at that subject I also might taken an exam in P.E. and I am quite good in goal at football.

I think the new exams are good ones they do not put people in categorys like some people were put in o-levels and others in c.s.e. and I think everyone should take the same exams.

I think I would rather not take them, but if I didn't I wouldn't get anywere in this world today.

I think that the G.C.S.E. is a good idea because if someone is more intellagent than someone else they can answer the more easier questions.

I think that this exam is better than C.S.E. and G.S.E. because some people would be put in for the top exam when they are not good enough, and

G.C.S.E. - THROUGH STUDENTS' EYES.

should be put in for the other exam. This exam gives good chances to the people who are not so good.

I think that more children should get further with the new system because you can chose to do the easy or the hard questions according to your ability.

1 of my sisters has just taken 10 o levels and she passed them all she dosn't think that the new system will work.

I am afraid that at the moment I know very little about this school's present examination system. However, I am sure that the new G.C.S.E. exam is a great improvement. From what I know of this new exam, it seems that it gives people of different intelligence to put their capabilities to their full use. Also, having one exam instead of two ('O' level and C.S.E.) rubs out all possibilities of unlucky 'border-line cases'. I am naturally worried about the exams, but not too much.

I think that the examination system would be slightly improved if, as well as taking an exam, pupils had their previous work checked over and marked. This would reduce the chance of bad marks if an exam went wrong.

I don't know a lot about this all I know is that my thought's would be, I would be very concerned about it I'm not to keen on G.C.S.E's and 'A' levels but I think it is a good idea so if you are quite cleaver you will get a job quickley.

My first thoughts on the new exam is why do you need a new exam when the old system works perfectly well. My brother has just done 9 'O' levels and passed them very well. If they are good enough for him they're good enough for me.

I think when I have my examinations I will be dead scard. I will soon not be scerd then. I think the new idear isbeter then the old one, in faked its brillyont. The old one must of been a lote more fritend becoase two is much wars then one. (remedial pupil).

113

G.C.S.E. - THROUGH STUDENTS' EYES

Comments from third year pupils, aged 13 - 14

With this new change even if you're not very good at a subject you get the same chance as the people who are good at the subject. In CSEs and GCEs everyone is split up into two groups. I don't know why we should do exams, why can't we have our grades based on our year's work. In an exam I'm always stuck for a difficult answer, and sometimes for an easy answer.

I feel that the G.C.S.E. willbe a better exam because then nobody will be dissapointed about not getting picked to do a higher intelligence level exam.

On the whole exams are a good idea, because it shows the teacher what your capable of and it shows yourself what you can do.

I think the change in most ways will be better, as before, with G.C.E. and C.S.E. the pupils were being split into different levels of education.

Also everyone will be working for the same thing which could make it easier for the teachers.

I think that this change isn't such a good one. The main reason for my thoughts are to do with satisfaction, and the satisfiaction you can get from passing a paper well. If everyone takes the same paper then obviously the less clever ones will not get so much satisfaction from failing or getting a low mark than getting a top mark on even a very low paper.

I think it's a very good change because it's not easy to know what exam you think you are capable of doing.

I think the new system is a good idea in the way that the tutor does not choose which examination he or she thinks is best for you to sit. though usually their decisions are accurate. Though, in the new system this problem does not occur as everyone takes one examination instead of being split into C.S.E. and G.C.E. groups.

G.C.S.E. - THROUGH STUDENTS' EYES.

From what I understand, I approve of the G.C.S.E. I think it will be easier for both teachers and pupils. I think it is nice to know that everyone will be doing the same exam, and so everyone is trying to reach the same goal.

On the whole I think that G.C.S.E. is better than the two exams.

I think they're a good idea, it saves deciding which exam to take. I dont like the idea of me and all the 3rd years having to play pigs but then someone will have to so why not us?

Although I think it is a good idea, I'm a bit worried by the fact that we are the first year to take G.C.S.E. as there are nearly always problems with something new. Adding to that, I think that the teachers strike will have caused the preparation for G.CSE. to be not as thorough as it could have been.

Anyway, overall I think it is a good idea, but I think that exams are a bad way of assessing someones work, because some people get very nervous about exams, and cannot work up to full standard - I think that the assesment of your work should be taken over the whole year, and not in end-of-term exams.

I think that G.C.S.E. would be better than the old system if everybody followed the same course instead of 2 separate courses. I seriously think that many people don't like exams, as they make you feel nervous and this soemtiems affects your performance in exams.

What do you I think about the change? - it's a difficult question to answer really. For the teachers it will be slightly easier as they won't have to decide who does G.C.E. and who does C.S.E. It may also be easier for the people who mark the papers. Instead of them having to mark two different question sheets there will only be one.

Examinations generally? - obviously they are an essential part of school life and although many people don't particularly like them, I do.

<u>Comments from third year pupils, aged 13 - 14   2)</u>

G.C.S.E. - THROUGH STUDENTS' EYES

I think that the new idea of grading is a good idea, because it gives people a better chance of passing the exam, whereas, in the old exam they may not get a pass grade.
It particularly helps the people, who, are bright enough to pass the exam, but don't because they become very nervous.
As the pass grades are lower it means that if they get an F or a G they will pass instead of fail.

I think that this change is better than the old system because everybody has the same chance at the question's set. And it has a wider range for the very intelligent and the not so intelligent People. If $\underline{F}$ is the average grade above F would be A very good grade.

It is a possibility that the G.C.S.E. exam will be more difficult, as F is the average mark. The G.C.S.E. must include the more difficult aspects of both other exams, but I think that the new marking system will probably be better because on the G.C.E. and C.S.E. there are 5 pass grades and anything below that is a fail, but with the G.C.S.E. you know exactly what the average mark is, and I think there might be more chances of passing the exam as there are more categories.

I think it may be discouraging for many people to work hard and gain what may seem a low grade. If the adverage grade were, for instance, 'D' it would seem more balanced. If 'F' is the adverage the marking is very biased in favour of higher achievers while a great many people will be left with no qualifications. I don't think that this new system will widen any opportunities in fact it will probably narrow them.
To me it seems that some people with outstanding practical abilities who need a certificate of compitence in such subjects as Maths and English may well be penalised by the suggested gradings.

I think the change to the new system is good because it means that if, in the old systen a teacher decided to enter a pupil for a G.C.E. when he or she would have been better off taking a C.S.E. the pupil might do badly and

G.C.S.E. — THROUGH STUDENTS' EYES

get an un-graded mark where as if they had been put in form the C.S.E. they would have got a proper pass grade like a 2 or 3.
In the new systen however everyone takes the same examination so these mistakes cannot be made and the pupil will obtain a proper grade even if it is only an F or G. I think therefore that the new examination is better for borderline cases where the teacher could not decide whether to enter a pupil for G.C.E. or C.S.E.

I think that perhaps there should be a few more grades below the average because although this system shows how good people above average are it does not show how well (or badly the people below average have done).
I also think that because people are so used to having only 5 pass grades they will think if they get a 'D', for instance, they have not done very well, but they will have done very well because 'D' is above the average grade.

I think that the G.C.S.E. system is better because all pupils will be following the same syllabus in a subject. This should make it easier for pupils to switch from one grade to another. Whereas in the old system it was more difficult to change from CSE to GCE and vice versa as the syllabus is different.
Another reason why I think it is better is that some employers think that CSE is not a proper qualification.

Comments from fourth year pupils, aged 14 - 15:

The continuous assessment allows people who want to get a good grade do so without having to take exams, as some people get very nervous and forget important information when everything relys on a good exam result. Also the present system for 'O' level you could do excellent class work and homework for two years and then get a bad exam result because you were nervous and forget things.

I don't think that the idea of Oral exams is a very good one because, many people don't like speaking and this could make them get a low result.

I like this change because you can do your very

G.C.S.E. - THROUGH STUDENTS' EYES

best work throughout the fourth and fifth years. I wish that I could do this exam because I get very nervous when sitting down in the hall to do a written exam.

I think that the G.C.S.E. exam is better because the work that the pupils do during the fourth and fifth year will seem more importtant.
I think the oral exam is good, because people have to talk a lot when they leave school but it is not a very good idea for shy people because they may not do as well as they would in a G.C.E. or C.S.E. exam.

I think this new exam will give the once C.S.E. people, a new surge of confidence. They won't be put in a 'thick' category.

Continuous assesment means your course work will also go towards your final marks so that even if you make a mess of your exam you have something to fall back on.

I do not like the idea though that you also have to depend on the oral part of the exam because if you are very self-consicious about talking in front of many people this could be a problem.

I think that the G.C.S.E. is a good idea rather than 'O' level and c.S.E. seperately, because if you fail the 'O' level you still have an examination result in C.S.E. It is a good idea to have continuous assessments because you might not do your exam very well because of being nervous and forgeting things or making a Mistake and Making a Whole Muck-up of it. But Oral exams for shy people or people who cannot put out their ideas easily may not be such a good idea.

In my opinion, continuous assesment is a disadvantage because very few people can produce their best work all through the year. Every person has their ups and downs, some may not find out the importance of their course work untill, in my own case, near hte end of the fourth year. I would rather spend $2\frac{1}{2}$ hours in an exam situation Oral exams is a better idea but totally useless. Every one can speak and everyone can fake a posh accent but those who

G.C.S.E. - THROUGH STUDENTS' EYES

can't well hard luck.

One proplem with this exam is that some teachers assessment may be of a higher standard.

The G.C.S.E. would be better because I think people would end up with a fairer exam result as some people are good at class work but not very good in exams.
Oral exams are good because whatever job you go into people are going to have to speak and they may make you more confident.

I am not for this change in examination as it will mean if someone was skiving or away from school they wouldn't pass the exam. Also if they have an arguement at home they won't have a very good mark.

This is a good idea as it will make people work hard throughout the year and not when exams are about to take place.

The continuous assessment through the fourth and fifth year may help people get better grades. With the system now people sometimes do not pay attention during classes which means they miss work and get themselves into trouble. If they know all their work is going to be put in their exam they may try harder instead of messing aobut during lessons then looking things up a couple of day before the exam at the eno of the school.
The oral exam would be alright for confident speakers, but the shy, quiet person would may not do so well.

I think that working throughout the year towards an exam mark is a good idea. I like this because if you don't work towards an exam you have done 2 years work for nothing if you have a bad day when the exam comes.

I believe it's a good idea because if you have to sit in the exam hall and just wirte out the exam them alot of people get scared and can't think of what to do until the exam is over.

When contiunous assesment is done through the year it should incourage the people who want to pass the exam to produce better work and to

119

G.C.S.E. - THROUGH STUDENTS' EYES

try harder.

I think the new exam is a good idea because i) continuous assessment will encourage you to work during the year, trying to achieve a high exam standard and when the written exams come then you will know what standard you are expected to acheive.
Oral exams are a good idea because they prepare you for the outside world where you will need to comunicate frequently.

I would prefer to do the old exams because you get a choice of the standard requirred.

I think that this is not a very good idea because if someone is away they have to catch up with their work and it will seem very hard.

Comments from Fifth year pupils - aged 15 - 16:

Unnecessary, and should be abolished in place of small tests each month.

This is true in some ways but not in others. I suffer badly with hayfever and usually when I take exams my eyes are streaming and I'm all stuffed up. But it is good because you need to have some thing to work for or I think people wouldn't work hard if they knew that there was going to be no exams.

I don't think that they should be abolish in place of something else which may be worse.

A necessary evil because sometimes people are good at classwork but when it comes to examinations their mind goes blank or they worry about what they will get.

I do agree with No.1 because it is a useful way of assesing what you are or are not capable of. It tests how well you understand things and have remembered them over the two years that you have studied a certain subject. It can compare you ability on a certain subject in comparrision with other people.

I agree with No.2. in the way that exams are necessary but I do not agree with exams in another sense which is that most exams are set

G.C.S.E. - THROUGH STUDENTS' EYES

in the summer whereas people with hayfever like myself sit there with their eye and nose running like taps and sneezing which can distract other people as well.

Exams are unnecessary, and should be abolished and put in place of...., Well, if they were going to get abolished I think they should be replaced with small, monthly tests to see what have remembered and understood.

I agree that they are a useful way of assessing what you have learnt but this is only the teachers way.

I think they are a necessary evil because they are the most accurate way of telling teachers and employers how many brains you have but it is too much to put your life on a few examinations.

Exams are unnecessary and should be abolished in place of many small tests. if you progress enough during the year then you should pass.

I agree that examinations are useful because, it is a good way of assessing what you have learnt, but it shouldn't be just the exam marks what pass you. The whole courses work should be taken into account as well as the exam marks. You could have a bad day and fail the exam but your course work could be excellent. Exams are a good thing but I think that the course work should be taken into account with the final percentage added up. But if they are abolished the monthly tests should take their place.

I agree with this because its' the only way to show what people have learnt.

I agree with this because I feel its' necessary for you to do the examination but I think its' an evil because it divids people up into sections.

I think that they are a quite useful way of finding out what you have learnt although some people do not do very well in exams but good classwork.

Unnecessary and should be abolished in place of short tests every so often and marks are added up

G.C.S.E. - THROUGH STUDENTS' EYES

Unnecessary, and should be abolished in place of...Teachers giving a grades work all through the years.

Unnecessary and should be abolished in place of. your teacher giving you a grade on how well you have done during your years work. Examinations are not a useful way of assesing what you have learnt because a pupil can be brainy during their lessons and do really well but panic and forget everything when it comes to the exam and do badly.

Exams are Evil but not necessary. Evil yes, necessary no. I don't think it makes any difference to whether you can survive or not a small bit of paper is no help. Work should be graded through the year.

Yes, I agree I cann't see any other sensible way of assesing somebodies ability. But I think the course work she have something to do with the final Mark, about ½ the Marks.

Unnecessary, and should be abolished in place of.. small monthly tests.

Unnecessary, and should be abolished in place of... course work.

I agree with number one examinations are a useful way of assessing what has been learnt. It tells the teacher if you are intelligent, and it tells the employers if you're intelligent. I don't think exams should be abolished. It is sensible to keep exams.

I think it is a good way of assessing what you have learnt because in someways you have something showing employers etc. the qualifications you got and how well you did in school.

Exams are a useful way of assessing what you have learnt because you can do all the work during the term's and then write what you have learnt in the exam.

Exams are a necessary evil. They are necessary but they are not evil because if you want to get a job you have got to have qualifications.

G.C.S.E. - THROUGH STUDENTS' EYES

If the exams were abolished employers wouldn't know if you were intelligent but there should also be a character study to see if you are reliable, honest and able to work.

No because you may have a bad day during the exams. No they are not necessary and could be ecchanged for course work. Unnecessary and should be abolished in place of monthly tests and coursework teacher could give grade.

Unnecessary and should be abolished in place of monthly tests which would take place in your classroom.

the problem is that some people 'crack-up' when it comes to exams, thus giving them an unfair grade.

There should be exam but not in there present form. There shouldn't be 'O' or CSE' type exams but exams at the end of each year, as we do at the moment is a good idea.

Exam are necessary as people will have the chance to 'shine' but the years work <u>must</u> be taken into judgement as some people can't work under an exam.

Comments from Sixth formers - aged 16 - 18:

The combining of the two exams into one seems, at first glance, to be a good idea. Staff will have their pupils all on the same track and eventually, after the two years course - aiming for the same goal. The work can be planned throughout the terms without interuption, which may in some cases set pupils back. As the jump from 'O' to 'A' level is already quite high, how will the future candidate cope?

To have one exam that everyone takes at the same level seems to me to be a lot better idea than to have two. There is too much prejudice regarding CSEs at present and whether or not they are regarded by the many as equivalent, if you acquire a C.S.E. grade 1, is controversial. A new exam will put an end to this controversy. I, for one, wouldn't like to be one of the guinea pigs for the new exam. It may result in many problems and to be the first to take it

G.C.S.E. - THROUGH STUDENTS' EYES

seems to me to be rather a risk to take. I am glad that I have got my 'O' levels out of the way. The danger, I think, in the new exam is that past grades, particularly C.S.E. grades, acquired by the year before the new 16+ exam comes into existance, may become useless. Employers will become used to the new grades and therefore disregard the old ones.

I don't know how the gradings going to work but it seems to me that people with lesser ability are going to get grades like D and E whereas before with the C.S.E. they would have been get 1's and 2's. Surely after two years work this does not seem to be much of an achievement. Basically, though, I think 16+ is a good idea but I'm glad I haven't got to do it.

I think that a new joint exam would be a good idea, in the sense that it would perhaps make subjects more interesting and therefore give the pupils more incentive to work. But on the other hand, a new joint exam might hold back certain pupils who need the 'O' level syllabus to push them to their true capability.

Having just passed nine G.C.E. exams in the fifth form, I feel that I am bound to be biased towards the old system of two different sets of exams. Without the G.C.E. and the knowledge that I was working solely against the top people in the country, I doubt whether I would have worked so hard and would have settled for just a fairly good grade.

On economic terms the G.C.S.E's are a good idea. They will cut down the extra costs of dealing with two different sets of boards, and the organisation of dealing with two sets of exams.

However, I feel that they will promote an even greater feeling of apathy amongst those who would have done C.S.E's than I witnessed last year. They will feel that there is no point in doing this exam, as they will only get low grades, compared to the high grades of those who would have done G.C.Es.

The old system was long overdue for a restructuring, although I feel that the expense of buying new textbooks and organising the new system could have waited until there were less demands on the school system than there are at the moment.

Having just got my 'O' levels and C.S.E. exams I have come to the conclusion that the existing exam system is unfair. I think this because by having ones two very different exams, pupils are segregated at the age of 14 according to their so-called "intelligence".

I don't think its fair that children of the same school, the same age etc., are bracketed off into these two very rigid groups.

I think all exams are wrong anyway because they dont test real intelligence or real knowledge of a subject. People can pass an exam with no enthusiasm or knowledge of a subject and get a good grade. i think it would be much fairer if a continual assesment and oral exams were put into action.

I took only 'O' levels in the fifth year, but had friends who felt humiliated because they thought they had been entered for too many C.S.Es, and so their intelligence "undermined". It was not clear to the people taking the exams that the C.S.E. set-up was often better (assesment _over_ the course etc), and perhaps the new system will incorporate better methods of examination than the usual two-hour examination panic.

All sorts of prejudices build up between different "types" of people, from about the second year in a comprehensive. The "C.S.E. or 'O' level"system, often imagined as the "thicky of swot" system, only secures these prejudices. With so many students, it is very difficult to get rid of the traditional "setting" system, but perhaps people with a common aim - a G.C.S.E. grade - may feel more at home with each other.

However, I thought the system of 'O' levels and C.S.E's was adequate as long as the pupils were dealt with fairly by the teachers; which I think we were here. It meant that you could take a mixture of two exams (or duel entry for safety) depending on your ability and understanding of each particular subject. Rather than the old,

G.C.S.E. - THROUGH STUDENTS' EYES

totally corrupt system of 'streaming', where either you were in stream 1 or not. I don't see the need for combining 'O' level and C.S.E. although presumably there are many sides to the arguement.

However, I disagree with any exam system anyway, which makes me rather hypocritical to judge or to suggest alternatives. But if there must be exams for very young people to centre their lives around while trying to survive maximum pressure, and hoping that on the one day out of two years worth of work they will perform well, then, I think the "16+", is not better than the present system.

The present system is too rigid and inacurate, schools are often unwilling to double enter classes occasionally formulated on convenance and not ability. I hope a more 'open' exam could eliminate these problems, which are often the cause of animosity and devision within the social structure of a school year.

I found the 'O' level and C.S.E. system very biased. You had to be either an 'O' level candidate or a C.S.E. candidate if you wore a borderline case you always seemed to be put in for c.S.E. so full potential was not always realised.

Combining the two examinations into one examination is a very good and logical idea which should give pupils an opportunity to do better than they may previously have done. It will begin to eliminate the feeling of some being intelligent while others are hopelessly stupid as similar courses will be sat. It should ideally bring back some of the equality intended in education.

My main reason for giving the examination my support is that it would prevent the discrimination, which today I feel exists between the people who have taken C.S.E. and 'O' level exams. By that I mean that many people still presume that people who take C.S.E are generally less academically minded than those who take 'O' level.

I have taken examination's at C.S.E. and 'O'

G.C.S.E. - THROUGH STUDENTS' EYES

level and find that in a few subjects taken at C.S.E. meant I had to do more work, such as projects.

I think that the idea of a joint exam is generally a good one. It would stop catagorisation between those participating in C.S.E's and those taking 'O' levels, and everyone would feel more equal with each other.

Taking a joint exam would also mean everyone would sit it at the same time, therefore having the same amount of preparation time, and the 'O' level candidates would be relieved of the usual chaos and excitement at the end of C.S.E's interupting their working progress.

Three months ago, I saw my 'O' levels at school. I now feel that 'O' level exams really only exist to test the memory of the student. In fact in only one exam I can think of, intelligence and intellectuality are actually required to pass the exam. That exam is English 'O' level.

I think it would be a good idea to replace c.s.e. and 'O' level exams with one exam. Before a child is told wether they will be doing either C.S.E. or 'O' level they are in a classroom with everybody else who are unsure of what exam they will be taking. This creates a lot of rivalry amongst the pupils who are all starting to take the higher exam.

Those chosen for 'O' level may decide that they are the elite and no longer need to try hard as they will automatically pass. Those selected to take CSE exams may say to themselves that they have no hope and are the failures of the school thus causing them to give up with their work.

It was a totally pointless idea to have two separate exams, from the point of view of those who had to take both in one subject, and due to all the confusion, paper work and money involved. In many subjects, the syllabus for the 'O' level varied quite widely from the CSE, meaning extra work for those dual-entered; people had to pay for the privilege of safeguarding their results, and I believe it a

127

G.C.S.E. - THROUGH STUDENTS' EYES

common practice for schools to dual-enter some of their best pupils, merely to make the school's CSE results look better. The two periods of examinations were also unnecessary - people had to take CSE's when they should have been working for 'O' levels, and the number of examinations that people who were dual-entered in a lot of subjects had to sit was crazy. Thus, I think it is indeed a far better idea to merge the two into the GCSE.

I also feel that the parents who prefer the traditional 0/CSE system could make it very difficult for this change.

A major produce of the separate examinations (CSE and GCE) is that the students are separated in to two categories; the academic students takings GCEs and the not-so academic students taking CSEs. The segragation can be the main cause of many disruptions in the school life. For example: many students degrade their fellow students with names, purely because they are taking the 'easy' CSEs. These names may eventually lead into a fight. The influences of the new examination is that it will create harmony between the two intelligences, by closing the gap between them.

The main disadvantage is the fact that the teachers are more involved with the marking and assessments. This could lead to favourism and subjective marking, as opposed to objective marking in the GCEs.

In my opinion the new system would decrease the number of suicide victims as every one will recieve an exam pass.

My opinion of the proposed change, is that I believe the system of the G.C.S.E. will be more unfairer than the 'O' and C.S.E. The reason I believe this is because the 'O' level has been specially adapted for people who are highly academic, while the CSE is designed for pupils of less academic ability, and so these exams because they are specially designed means more higher grades can be obtained in each case of 'O' and CSE. Also it means that pupils taking CSE have the chance to gain high grades which are equivalent to 'O' level, even though they

G.C.S.E. - THROUGH STUDENTS' EYES

would not have the ability to take part in this exam.

My opinion of the proposed change is that I would preffer to keep the current 'O' and CSE exams. This new G.C.S.E. system seems to be harder. I think it does offer too much for a normal C.S.E. candidate. This exam, should be offered to those who are capable of getting a high 'O' level grade only. CSE candidates may not be up to the standard struggling through the course work, and later getting a very low grade or even being ungraded. The current CSE, at least offers candidates a chance to get a high grade in that exam.

The changes which will be taking place in the examination will change the face education. This is what we have been told on the television. The new examination the G.C.S.E. is an affiliation of the two old systems the G.C.E. which is known as the 'O' level and the C.S.E. A change can only be for the better in my opinion as the descrimination between 'O' levels and C.S.E. is very bad. We are told at school repeatidly that C.S.E. is just as good as 'O' level 'C' pass. If this is the case why is it that people on the borderline are pressured if not forced into going into the C.S.E. examinations. I hope that with the new examination the dividing line between C.S.E. and 'O' level will disappear.

I have taken C.S.E's and 'O' levels and on the whole I think that the way C.S.E. examination are set is the better of the two. Having your work marked throughout the year lets the pressure of an examination drop. I hope that the new examination will change attitudes and lead to a better more equal exam which will be better for all concerned.

I have only taken c.S.E. and 16+ exams so far. I think the C.S.E. give the people who do not do well in exams a much better chance of passing, because there is more oral work and also the classwork pays a greater part in the examination. From what my friends have told me the G.C.E. is on one day and if you're feeling unwell that day and you have an exam you are not likely to pass.

G.C.S.E. - THROUGH STUDENTS' EYES

I think that the new examination taking place of G.S.E. and C.S.E. may prove to be a good move. It seems that as the new examination - the G.C.S.E., takes into account the coursework done during the two years of working through the actual syllabus, it will take off a lot of pressure from the proposed candidates during the actual exam. I personally took the G.C.E. exam last year and failed miserably, but this year I have been lucky and have been given the chance to try again, but this time putting more work into the syllabus and showing myself a sheer determination not to be defeated again.

I believe that if the boards are going to combine the GCE and the C.S.E. examinations the should arrange the marks in such a way that evenbody who workss passes.

I feel that the change will lead to a long awaited imporvement in the exam system. Firstly it removes the lengthy exam period and will scale all students on the same grading system. I do however feel that the average has been set too low.

Having taken only 'O' levels I obviously have no complaints about the 'old' system. However, I know that many students feel second best if they have CSE's because despite the 'equivalent' idea CSE is widely regarded as a second best exam.

The new G.C.S.E. examinations appear to be a very good idea since they establish a common basis upon which examinations can be viewed. I feel that the present system does not really do this and having taken three dual entries in my time I cannot feel that they are in any way comparable, although I do know that a C.S.E. is recognised as an 'O' level pass. I find the proposals for continous assesment and oral tests for all subjects most appealling since the present system of having to regurgate everything in one go not only penalises those who do not have excellent memories, especially in subjects like history, but also does not account for minor fluctuations in a pupils life which may affect performance on the examination day. Continuous assesment can overcome this.

The proposed change will be beneficial to all pupils as:
(a) It will eradicate the problems and cost involved when choosing G.C.E. C.S.E. or both.
(b) It will reduce the number of boards needed to operate the system;
(c) It will examine the whole spectrum of abilities giving all pupils equal opportunities;
(d) It will help employers who found it hard to understand that a C.S.E. 1 equals an 'O' level pass;
(e) It will take away the unnecessary traditions associated between the old grammar school and secondary modern system and emphasise the comprehensive system;
(f) It will combine the benefits of both the G.C.E. and C.S.E. system;
(i) C.S.E. - projects, oral examinations;
(ii) G.C.E. - practical tests, data response and the traditional essay;
(g) It may reduce pressures on teachers.

I took 'O' levels in June 1984, and I remember it as the worst period of my life. My own experience has allowed me to see the problems involved in the present GCE/CSE system. I feel that the change to the new GCSE exam could only be for the better. The first problem with the current system is that there are two separate exams with different names. It seems to defeat the principles of comprehensive education that all pupils are given equal opportunities until the exam system differentiates between them at 16. I think it is grossly unfair that the result of two years work should be judged on a candidate's performance in two or three written papers. At 'O' level no credit is given for the coursework the candidate has produced over the period. There is also little or no consideration given to the circumstances under which the exams are taken. Anything from personal problems to the weather may affect a candidate's performance on the day of the exam. June is the worst time of year to take exams. It is usually very hot then and many students suffer from hayfever. Little is known about the marking patterns of the exam papers and there is apparently no clear borderline to distinguish between the various grades. I also have little faith in the complaints procedure nor in the appeal's board. I felt as if my fate

G.C.S.E. - THROUGH STUDENTS' EYES

was in someone else's hands.

My opinion of the change from two examinations, C.S.E. and G.C.E. to one examination, G.C.S.E. is that I don't see why the system, which has gone on for so many years has to be changed. There may be some pupil, who is not able to cope with G.C.E. level of work, so is put in to a C.S.E. group, so he/she has an equal chance of passing the exam, unlike in the new system, where there is only one exam you can do.

Personally I don't think the change is a very good idea as different people have different standards of work. I think that 2 examinations are better because if you aren't as bright as other children you can be entered for the one that isn't so hard.

I don't really understand why the system has to be changed because there will always be someone who isn't bright enough or intelligent enough to be able to do the new G.C.S.E. At the moment people stand more chance of getting some kind of result with the C.S.E.

I think that the proposed change will be better. This is partly better because with the present GCE and CSE systems it is difficult to change people from one group to another, part of the way through the cource. This happened to me in English because I was on a 'O' level group, and then the teachers decided that I was not good enough to take the exam, so I was dropped to a CSE group. I then had to try and catch up all the CSE syllabus work.

As a person who doesn't tend to do herself justice in exams, I think that a system which included continuous assessment would be much better. Obviously a system of total continuous assessment would be equally unfair to those people who do as well or even better in exams than expected, and so, as in the new exam system, a compromise should be reached. This means that the result of two years of study does, not depend only on a few hours of exams at the end of the course. People do have bad days, and only one slip can mean the difference between a job or the dole; or, at 'A' level, it can mean the loss of a university place.

The comments from sixth formers reflect the experiences of students from nineteen different schools, including independent schools, schools from rural and urban areas who enter a large Open Sixth containing 400 students and they are particularly revealing, thoughtful and thought provoking. The effect of the dual examination system on pupils' relationships emerge clearly, and whilst there are varying degrees of opinion, most students appear to see the existence of this duality as incompatible with the comprehensive school. Some of the comments consider the wider issues in some detail, and perhaps there is a need, in getting the new system off the ground, to do just this. The experts designing the system must not become so pre-occupied with the mechanics and techniques, the constitutions and procedures that the fundamental purpose of the reform is forgotten. Perhaps the students' comments are a reminder of the need for a unified system of examinations in a unified secondary school system.

REFERENCES

(1) The Hewett School, Norwich. The author is grateful to the students concerned for their co-operation and response.

Chapter Seven

A PLAN FOR ACTION

One of the main concerns felt by teachers charged with the responsibility for launching the G.C.S.E., is how to meet the need for effective and efficient implementation. Whatever the deficiencies of the new system, whatever reservations there may be on the part of the professionals, there is a consensus that carefully planned implementation must have high priority. This is easier stated than done. Compared with earlier changes in the examination system, schools face a very different climate today. The transition from the old School Certificate to the General Certificate of Education affected a relatively small minority of the school population, being aimed at the top 20% of the ability range. The extension of the G.C.E. beyond that figure was a gradual process. The Certificate of Secondary Education, when launched in the early 'sixties, certainly extended the target group to another 40 per cent of the secondary school population, and although this affected larger numbers, it was again a more gradual process. At that time, the education system in general, and schools in particular, were in an expansionist situation. There was an air of optimism, a climate which favoured reform, and a general feeling of support towards schools and teachers. Although resources were never plentiful, the political will to improve the system was there. Politicians were supportive rather than hostile and so were the parents. Society in general, whilst showing high expectations of what the schools could and should deliver, was generally perceived to be pro-education, for the schools, and for the teachers. Above all, there was investment in education - governments and l.e.a's were willing to spend money to improve the system.

It was against such a background that the

134

A PLAN FOR ACTION

enormous amount of goodwill shown by teachers, was reflected in thousands of hours of voluntary unpaid work, as board and panel members which helped C.S.E. off the ground. The situation is very different today. The same government which has decided in favour of a single examination system, is also hostile to the education service, or at the very least, is perceived to be against the teaching profession. Attempts to link salary proposals with the assessment of teachers initiated by Sir Keith Joseph, have met with fierce opposition, and with strikes and other industrial action on a large scale; the major teachers' unions, in varying degrees, are highly critical of government policy and government action. There is a resource crisis in the schools, which, in recent years has, itself been a cause of the turbulences of industrial action inside the schools. Although the examination system as such, has so far been largely exempt from industrial action, it would be totally wrong to assume that there is the same degree of support for change as in earlier days. Although the teaching profession strongly favoured, and still favours, this important examination reform, there is less support for the manner in which it has been launched. The response to the national criteria requirements has been one of resigned acceptance rather than positive enthusiasm. Teachers have often seen it as part of a centralist philosophy, but have, with some reluctance, accepted that a price has to be paid if the reform is to be launched at all. The schools are under continuous pressure not only to perform better, but to communicate in greater detail and with greater frequency, what they are about. Such trends are inescapable, and point powerfully towards the need for a plan for action to explain the changes to parents, employers, politicians, and to the whole body of external agencies in any way connected with, or bearing on, school life. In suggesting such a plan there is a need for realism: such realism suggests that the manner, quality and timing of any external relations programme will vary according to individual schools and local authorities. Neither the institutions concerned, nor the people who work in them can be pushed too far, and too fast along a particular path taken by the centre. On the other hand, failure to have any programme at all will simply mean that other agencies will fill the gap and appoint themselves as the spokesmen for G.C.S.E. adding further to the problems of those who have

A PLAN FOR ACTION

the task of implementing it.
There is need for an external relations policy both in a general and in a specific sense. The general public, however defined, needs to have a clear perception and understanding of the changes which are about to happen. The questions why change? How will the changes be made and when will they be effective? need answering. To some extent, the need to create a general sense of awareness that the system will change, will be met by publicity and communication aimed at the professional educators, but it is as well to bear in mind that the language used by professionals is not always easily understood, or well received, by the man or woman in the street. In devising a plan for action, the need to paint a widely accepted and easily understood, general picture needs to be borne in mind. In defining target groups to be reached, parents and employers should have high priority, and suggestions made later in this chapter outline a programme of action for them.

However, important work will also have to be done by reaching specific groups of professionals not immediately concerned with the implementation of G.C.S.E., but sufficiently closely connected with the education of young people to require accurate and easily accessible information presented in a reasonably concise form. Such groups are identified as follows:-

1. <u>Teachers in primary and middle schools.</u>
Prior to transfer to the secondary stage, the existence of a public examinations system is known by and communicated to the pupils and parents by colleagues in these schools. Hence, they need adequate briefing, bearing in mind that the degree of priority which they can give to learning about the new system must be considerably less than that shown by their secondary colleagues, as their day to day work requires a different orientation.

2. <u>Local advisors and inspectors.</u>
These can clearly be expected to have much more detailed knowledge of both general trends, contents of syllabuses and both the general and specific national criteria required for their approval by the Secondary Examinations Council. They will also be the people who will, or should be, most acutely conscious of the need for adequate resource provision. However, it has to be recognised that senior local authority personnel will have a different perspective from individual teachers. They will be concerned with the need for

implementation in all schools in the whole area served by the l.e.a. On the one hand, such a wider perspective is essential to collate the needs of schools as they become apparent; on the other, the overview of advisors and inspectors can sometimes be itself a limiting factor, since the vast details which schools need to absorb and handle, cannot possibly be known by them. There is therefore, a need for understanding that the implementation of G.C.S.E., is a reciprocal rather than a hierarchial process. For an l.e.a. to boss schools about simply adds to the pressures and achieves very little.
3.   <u>Other professionals in the education service</u>.
     These fall into four groups:
(i) Chief Education Officers, their deputies and those who occupy the higher positions in the educational hierarchy will have neither the time, and may sometimes lack the inclination, to concern themselves with too much detail. They will expect sufficiently good briefing to make major policy decisions. Such decisions, e.g. the extent to which schools should be given facilities for opting for boards outside their region, the consequences of doing so on the release of teachers, on entry fees, and similar matters, are of vital concern to schools. Senior officers will therefore need to be particularly sensitive in the process of decision making as it affects the new system.
(ii) <u>Careers Officers and the Careers Service</u>.
     Major reorientation will be required here. Careers Officers grappling with the impact of large scale unemployment amongst school leavers, however well cushioned by the Youth Training Scheme, have their own pressures and many of them are sceptical about examinations as such as a passport to better jobs or any jobs at all. Consultation, participation, involvement and briefing will be required.
(iii) Junior administrative and clerical staff
     <u>in l.e.a. offices</u>.
     Such people should not be neglected. They will handle entry queries, queries concerning the payment of fees, and the more routine communications from the examination boards. There is a need for a public relations exercise to understand and communicate with such persons rather than take it for granted that they will automatically do what someone else expects, in launching a new system.
(iv) The other large group of professional requiring careful servicing are the <u>academic staff in higher and further education</u>. Although G.C.S.E. results

A PLAN FOR ACTION

bear no direct relationship to decision making on entries to universities, polytechnics, colleges of higher education, and other higher education institutions, all of which rely on 'A' level grades, they are nevertheless, looked at and form an important part of an applicant's profile. Sometimes a decision on grade requirements for entry to a particular course of study is affected by records at 16+. There has never been any doubt that young people with good 'O' level grades on an UCCA form have better prospects in the eyes of higher education selectors than those with a mixed bag of grades, and there is every reason to suppose that such policies will be maintained in the new examination system. However, the seven point grading scheme, the national criteria, and later, criteria referencing will present a new perspective for the world of higher and further education.

Teacher Training Institutions:

One sometimes hears criticisms that new entrants to the teaching profession are either not sufficiently briefed or even unaware of the major changes inherent in the examination system. Such criticisms are often ill founded. Nevertheless, they exist, and the introduction of the G.C.S.E. provides a new opportunity to establish closer links between the world of teacher education and the examination world, and that opportunity should be taken. Examination boards in particular, need to review their contacts with teacher educators and seek advice on the best method of servicing the institutions which train the teachers.

At the centre, Her Majesty's Inspectors, and civil servants of the Department of Education and Science, can be expected to have a thorough and detailed knowledge, but again, with a different perspective from that existing inside the schools. Both groups have a vested interest in ensuring that the reforms are implemented speedily and efficiently. There is however, a difference: the Inspectorate is independent of the Secretary of State, and can be expected to be not only aware of, but sensitive to the problems which schools will experience. There will therefore, be a need not only to contribute to the general debate, but to identify the nature and intensity of the problems, and appraise the decision makers at governmental level of the situation as it develops. The paramount need will be to recognise the need for flexibility, particularly as far as the implementation of national criteria is concerned. There is a need to distinguish on the one hand, between the broad canvas of the general criteria which is now largely accepted, and some subjective notions which subject experts, whether inspectors or teachers, display and which need to be set aside at a time of great pressure. The Inspectorate must report on the picture as it develops, and bearing in mind the tremendous variations between schools, must go out of its way to recognise the need for sensitivity and facility for individual approaches, as preferable to moving towards rigid uniformity and conformity. The same applies to civil servants who are charged to oversee the whole exercise. The success of the G.C.S.E., and its acceptance by many interests will depend on creating a consensus which does not yet exist. An educational world at odds within itself, with attempted diktats from central government, quarrelling with examination boards, is no recipe for reform. A deliberate move to understand, to seek agreement, and to publish what is agreed rather than what divides, is an essential requirement to create the confidence which the new system needs.

There are two further non-professional groups with a high stake in the whole examination business. These are the parents of students in schools taking the examination and the employers and their organisations, both at local and national level concerned with the recruitment of school leavers possessing the new qualification. In any plan for action, these two groups require the highest priority.

The expertise of providing the right information at the right time and in the right form, lies with the professionals and they cannot escape either the dilemma or the responsibility. The effective communicators will be the teachers in schools, whose workload is such that they cannot be expected to get a detailed programme off the ground themselves. The need is therefore, for an overall strategy requiring judgments as to who should be informed, in what manner, to what extent and at which times. The schools themselves will undoubtedly decide what can and should be done at school level. This point is further explored in the following pages, but it is as well to itemise the tasks which local education authorities will need to perform.

First and foremost, there is a need for an l.e.a. to have an overall policy and in particular, to give clear support to the examination group in whose area the authority is placed. This need not imply any limitations on the right of schools to opt

A PLAN FOR ACTION

for particular syllabuses and boards outside their regions. But local education authorities must see themselves as partners, at least to the same extent in which they joined with the C.S.E. boards, in accepting responsibility for implementation. The model here is that of the C.S.E. rather than the G.C.E. boards.

Secondly, the devising and operating of suitable training programmes, in conjunction with the examination boards, needs to be seen as a continuous process rather than an exercise which can be disposed of quickly by a few periodic meetings of teachers. The reforms are far reaching and fundamental, using new techniques of assessment and operating within a national framework; these are new dimensions which will grow, develop and become modified over the years. The only way in which l.e.a's can ensure high quality examining in their schools is to accept and further the notion that a training programme which continues over several years is essential and will have to form a major component of their in-service training.

Finally, there is no escaping the need for adequate financial provision by l.e.a's. The areas which require costing will include at least the following:
1. The school element.
    As previously mentioned, the cost of re-tooling will need to be estimated by each school, and a phased programme of making provision in calculating additional capitation allowances for the introduction and development of G.C.S.E. is essential.
2. The training element.
    This follows from what has been said above, and needs equal careful planning and costing. There is no chance of doing all that should be done prior to the introduction of G.C.S.E. in 1986. This however, in no way obscures the need for properly designed INSET programmes, carefully co-ordinated with what other agencies are doing. In 1986, only one year group secondary pupils entering their fourth year, will be concerned with the new examination. This gives more time to plan a proper strategy for the years to come, avoiding on the one hand, duplication with other agencies, and on the other, clearly reflecting the needs as identified at school level.
3. The communication element.
    High quality communication cannot and should not

A PLAN FOR ACTION

be conceived as an ad hoc procedure, with bits and pieces gleaned by the local press from meetings of education and school committees. L.E.A's need to sit down with their teachers to devise a proper programme for informing parents, employers in their locality, and the general public, as well as the other professional groups. Such a communication programme should include the servicing of lay members of local authorities.

The examination boards and groups will need no persuading of the need for a plan for action. All the signs are that they are aware of the need to reach the different target groups. Rightly, and inevitably, their immediate attention is concentrated on the schools who provide the clients, and the competitive element alone ensures that a liberal flow of information reaches the schools. All groups know that freedom of choice can mean larger entries, and the G.C.E. boards have always had a national perspective. At the same time, the need for the wider audience, as discussed earlier, must not be overlooked. The quality of publications aimed at schools, at other interests, the frequency of their appearance, the need to use language which may often have to be significantly different from customary usage, are matters for careful planning and sound policy making. All the signs are that the new examining groups are rising to the challenge and that there will be no shortage of publicity material.

The Secondary Examinations Council has a particular function to perform in presenting G.C.S.E at national level. However, the main job of publicity aimed at schools will have to be done by the examination groups, and the S.E.C. should see itself as the main co-ordinator of their activities, whilst emphasising its role as the main channel of communication between the groups and the Department of Education and Science, and especially the Secretary of State. This is a delicate and difficult task, which must not be underestimated. It is essentially a political, rather than a professional task, influenced by the personalities in office. The need is to separate the political from the professional issues, a process not readily understood, or accepted, by politicians. It means that S.E.C. publicity and public relations will often be influenced by the requirements of diplomacy, rather than the stance taken at a public platform.

Finally, the Department of Education and Science, whilst having a responsibility to communicate

A PLAN FOR ACTION

clearly and in easily readable form the decisions made by government is not the right body to communicate with parents at school level. Its first leaflet [1] on G.C.S.E., offered to schools for distribution, is a poor example of what is required. Such exercises are best left to the schools themselves.

Parents are of course best approached through their individual schools, and schools will wish to call briefing meetings as well as providing suitable material for their parents. The following basic information will need to be communicated to parents:

    The title of the new examination
    The subjects available
    The time at which G.C.S.E. examinations takes place
    Grading schemes
    Results, including details of times of publication
    Difference from G.C.E. and C.S.E. and advantages of the new examination
    Information concerning fees
    Policy regarding re-sits to improve performances
    Name of examination board/boards used
    Written, oral and continuous assessment procedures
    Acceptability of G.C.S.E. by users, particularly higher and further education and employers

Much material will best be prepared by individual schools with specific statements directed towards their own parents, but the examination boards themselves should provide a 'basic kit' for schools in their area to reduce workload, which could be used for a first essential distribution to parents, with a suitable covering letter provided by the schools.

The parents to be reached are all those whose boys and girls are starting courses in the autumn of 1986, i.e. those entering the fourth year of secondary education in that year, and all younger pupils, already in the school, as well as new entrants each autumn. It is suggested that it would be better to concentrate on these groups rather than call general meetings of parents to avoid confusion. Parents of older pupils specifically interested, could certainly be invited if interested, but their children will of course continue to take the existing examinations until 1988.

The timing of such an exercise at school level and the manner of presentation is extremely

A PLAN FOR ACTION

important. A useful plan for action is as follows:
1. Written communication sent to parents whose children will be taking the new examination, containing the basic information either as a specific publication or as part of a newsletter which many schools publish already. For 3rd years, the spring term or the early part of the summer term prior to entering the 4th year is a good time. If, because of pressure of school business, it has not been possible to reach such parents in the first half of 1986, the information should be supplied in the autumn term.
During 1987, further information can be supplied at intervals throughout the year, aimed at those who will then be third year pupils.
2. Spring and early summer in 1988, i.e. the period before G.C.S.E. is taken for the first time, will be a critical time, and a further brief communication indicating precise times, dates for written and oral exams and for the issue of results, and reminding parents of information supplied earlier, will be very useful and will do a great deal to foster the feelings of understanding and security which both parents and pupils need at this time.
3. In the summer of 1988, the first results will be available and will need evaluation. Here again, this provides scope for a suitable communication to parents, and results, which have to be published anyway, should be accompanied by suitable comment from the school.

In devising suitable publicity material, the need for clarity and quality in presentation, will be paramount. Inevitably, written material will be easiest to handle and easiest to communicate to many homes. However, a video presentation explaining the basic concepts of the examination and actually showing pupils at work, together with tapes showing the operation of oral examining, will do much to foster understanding. A typical parent/teacher meeting, arranged to follow the basic communication sent to parents earlier, could take the following form:
1. Brief exposition by the head or senior member of the school's staff on the school's policy on G.C.S.E.
2. A similar, fairly brief, statement by an official of an examination board or group indicating what examiners, assessors and moderators do and how results are arrived at.

A PLAN FOR ACTION

Here, mention of the appeals system will be well received.
3. A video presentation showing pupils preparing for or engaged in work to be assessed by the examination, will arouse considerable interest.
4. Exhibition of pupils' work, i.e. work in process, particularly that which will form the material for continuous assessment, will be of enormous value, if possible, accompanied by tape recordings of pupils training for the oral component of the examination. Such exhibitions and displays are an excellent accompaniment to the more formal part of the evening, allowing for an informal exchange once the expositions are finished. If pupils undertaking the work, are themselves in attendance explaining what they are about, the whole exercise becomes a stimulating and realistic public relations function with a professional touch.

Other variants which will be found useful on such evenings are as follows:
(a) the provision of an information desk with appropriate materials, manned by students as well as staff;
(b) an opportunity for individual consultation with key members of staff and examination officers.

A simple form inviting parents to leave their queries if they cannot be answered on the spot is a good way of monitoring trends in peoples' queries.
(c) Group discussions. Parents with particular interests in certain subject areas can be invited to join groups addressed by members of staff.
(d) Display of examination certificate and result slips. These will not be available until after the first examination takes place in 1988, but mock certificates and results slips, which will be available in draft form, again add an air of reality and expectation.

Parents are naturally interested in what happens to their child rather than the operation of systems, and the need is therefore to provide the kind of contact which relates the new examination to the individual child. This will be particularly important when it is realised that the common system contains alternative papers, a grading system where an F or a G is actually a pass, and new features such as criteria referencing. The statement that the system is designed to show pupils what they can do, rather than penalise them for what they do not know, needs to be developed and shown to exist in

A PLAN FOR ACTION

practice. There is no doubt that the grading system, as it stands at present, will provoke both disappointment and possibly disillusionment. Great care will therefore need to be taken in the public presentation of the whole system to avoid, or at least lessen, such feelings, and present the positive aspects of G.C.S.E. as the examination which gives everybody equal access and hopefully, equal opportunity. At the same time, there must be honesty - no examination system can ensure that everybody gets good results all the time, in every subject, every year. Both parents and pupils, as well as users, know this. The people who can do this best are the teachers in the secondary schools. In launching G.C.S.E., all local authorities and examination boards need to be very much aware of the great professional input that will be required, and the approach to the use of supply teachers, the provision of resources for material and the purposeful development of training element, will underpin the success of the examination if handled with sympathy and intelligence.

The provision of suitable information for primary, middle and other feeder schools, is no less important, although easier to handle since fellow professionals are affected. The following plan for action in approaching such institutions may be useful:

1. Provide the same material as used for parents, with a covering letter. The time to do this should be closely related to the time when pupils are allocated or opt for their new secondary schools, because it is then that interest is at its highest.
2. There should be additional information for primary and middle school teachers of a professional nature, relating particularly to:
(i) differentiated schemes and target groups;
(ii) the oral component and the extent to which it figures in various examinations;
(iii) continuous assessment.

The fact that oral English is a compulsory part of English should be highlighted.

3. An invitation to visit and meet secondary colleagues concerned with G.C.S.E. will enable useful feedback to take place.
4. A person to person link, particularly in the early years of launching G.C.S.E., will be useful and eliminate much misunderstanding. Such links do of course already exist in many schools, but where this is not the case, it is

A PLAN FOR ACTION

highly desirable that the specific person or persons co-ordinating the arrangements in a secondary school, should be known to the feeder schools.

5. Group or area meetings between primary and secondary colleagues in the first few years, as part of the INSET provision, will be highly desirable.

The local education authorities are equal partners with the teachers and examination boards in the enterprise. The paramount need is for professional co-operation and a professional dialogue between teachers, examination boards officials and local authority officers, especially subject advisers. Assuming that such officers see their task in assisting the teachers in the schools to do the job of implementing G.C.S.E., to help to identify and resolve problems, the resulting co-operation can and should be an enriching professional experience for both parties. Above all, the need is to avoid a hierarchial approach. Subject advisers should have a thorough knowledge of the syllabus content, of the assessment procedures in particular, and be able to advise on the solutions of problems which may arise as a result of operating the general or the subject specific crtieria. In the early stages, the existence of this criteria in the twenty subjects published so far, is likely to give rise to some problems, possible misunderstandings and even friction. It is important to recognise that the interpretation of what constitutes the criteria is a function of the examining boards themselves, with the Secondary Examinations Council acting as an overseer. As has already been shown, the criteria vary in the amount of detail, and the requirements according to different subject areas, and the flexibility which this provides should be used. Furthermore, in all subjects other than the twenty mentioned, the general criteria only applies and there is therefore a considerably greater element of discretion in making judgments, certainly until further specific criteria are published. Finally, the vast number of mode 2 and 3 syllabuses submitted by individual schools are to be approved by the examination groups, subject to sample scrutiny by the S.E.C. Subject advisers therefore need to become skilled specialists in the interpretation of the general and specific criteria, in the assessment procedures to be followed, and particularly in helping to train teachers in methods

A PLAN FOR ACTION

of oral examining and continuous assessment. Whilst many teachers, particularly those concerned with C.S.E., will already be acquainted with such techniques, it is important to appreciate that the numbers of teachers to be concerned will be vastly increased. In English alone, every candidate is required to be examined orally, and nearly all syllabuses approved need to have a continuous assessment element. This is an enormous task which needs to be clearly reflected in the INSET strategy of local education authorities.

There will also be a considerable impact on school organisation. Schools with large entries in C.S.E., English, which has usually had an oral component, or/and in subjects where oral examination has been an important element, are only too well aware of the great organisational problems which have to be solved. The same applies to the detailed arrangements necessary for practical examinations. Thus, general advisers and inspectors of local education authorities, need to study carefully the impact on school organisation during the main examination periods and act with sympathy and understanding in helping to launch the new system. The need is to design an INSET programme which concentrates on the essentials and spreads them across a wide professional field, identifying clearly those issues which will be of immediate and major concern to teachers implementing G.C.S.E. The following themes provide an outline programme for such a local INSET programme:

1. Knowing your syllabus - criteria for comparison.
2. Fitting syllabuses to students.
3. Differentiated schemes and different target groups.
4. Assessment procedures.
5. The new grading scheme - differences from previous schemes.
6. Resource considerations - estimated cost of re-tooling.
7. Administrative procedures, entry forms and fees.
8. Contact with examination boards and groups - exercising freedom of choice and/or sticking with your own group - advantages and drawbacks.
9. External relations, publicity and communications with parents and users.
10. Identifying further training components, as seen by the schools.

In implementing such an INSET training programme, the local education authorities will themselves need to develop a strategy for priorities, with G.C.S.E.

A PLAN FOR ACTION

occupying a high place. Neglect in this area will be costly in real terms in handling complications and complaints from all sources which can be avoided by intelligent planning and foresight, and a clear recognition of what needs to be done.

Lay members of education committees of local authorities and their sub-committees, are of course aware that a change in the examination system is to take place, but it would be fair to state that in all but exceptional cases, they have no detailed knowledge of the nature of the changes, nor of the tremendous tasks which the schools face in getting the new system off the ground. Among local councillors who do not serve on education committees there is even less knowledge, and some may be entirely unaware that the changes are already on our doorstep. To say this is not to be critical of the state of educational knowledge amongst elected councillors, but to recognise the need for informing them adequately as decision makers and holders of local purse strings. The magnitude of ensuring that local authority members are at least adequately briefed to ensure high quality decision making in matters relating to the G.C.S.E. should not be underestimated. The pressure on LEA members is such that the simple expectation that they should find time to learn all about G.C.S.E. in an ad hoc manner is not realistic. The continuing resource crisis in local authorities, the tensions between central and local government, the pay disputes in the public sector affecting not only teachers, but other local government officers and employees, are putting the whole machinery of local government under enormous strain. There are no simple answers to the dilemma of crowded agendas, long and frequent meetings and volumes of material to be read and digested. Nor can it be assumed that there is necessarily a great deal of sympathy for the change among many lay members; some would rather not have the change at all. Considerable numbers of Conservative councillors were opposed to what they saw simply as the abolition of the General Certificate of Education and highly critical of Sir Keith Joseph for initiating the change. Their voices may have been muted of late, but are sure to be raised whenever cost considerations impinge on their deliberations. Among Labour councillors, the principle of the change is usually welcomed, but the nature of its implementation by the government, and the fierce opposition to aspects of government policy in education sometimes means that controversy clouds issues and becomes an end in itself. The Alliance, as a new and emergent force in local government has yet to make a detailed policy statement on G.C.S.E., but the signs are hopeful that there is a readiness for a new approach, and new thinking.

The senior officers who serve lay members are themselves subject to enormous pressures, and it should not be overlooked that the Association of County Councils is on record in pressing the Secretary of State to postpone the start of G.C.S.E. for one year. Such a postponement, even if the Secretary of State accepts it, will not make any fundamental difference to resource provision, since the political situation is not likely to change nationally between 1986 and 1987. The task is therefore one of ensuring that members of local authorities are sufficiently well briefed on G.C.S.E. to recognise the fundamental nature of the change, its importance throughout the educational system, and the high priority which will need to be given to resource provision in this area. The challenge is to change what are often negative or indifferent attitudes, to positive acceptance and support for the change. The aim must be to create a positive climate among councillors, and this requires rather more than just pointing out the inevitable difficulties which such a change brings. Enlightened leadership on the part of the chief officers and their staffs, in co-operation with the teaching profession and the examination boards, can make a substantial contribution in promoting harmony rather than controversy; there is therefore a need to plan and implement a scheme of training for councillors.

This should begin by holding an early special meeting of the education committee of the local authority and followed by a day conference to enable the major issues to be addressed. The papers for such a conference should include suitable material published nationally, by the examination boards and on a sample basis, by the schools. It is neither necessary nor desirable that the whole twenty publications of the Department of Education and Science relating to national criteria should be handed to local authority members. However, the booklets on the introduction to the new system, on the operation of the general criteria, and one or two examples relating to a couple of subject areas, together with the general statements published by the examining groups in which the local authority is

A PLAN FOR ACTION

situated, should be prepared in the form of an information pack given to every member. A simple statement, setting out the main issues, and indicating the sources for obtaining further materials is essential. Such materials should certainly be available in each county hall, and a reference section dealing entirely with the introduction of the new examination system is highly desirable. This is best housed in the education department, to enable members of committees to have ready access.

The special meeting of the education committee to precede the conference should enable senior officers, and the teacher representatives to take a major part in initiating a discussion. It should be made clear that this is a briefing meeting, to enable productive discussion to take place at a conference specially arranged for members. Such a conference, whilst not being too large, should include a sufficient number of school teachers with particular responsibility for implementing the change, including heads, departmental heads, as well as younger teachers without specific responsibilities within the school hierarchy, but still faced with the task of getting the work done. Officials from the local examination boards, including those representing the group, should be invited. These should previously be asked to provide a stand where material is displayed in an attractive manner with personnel ready to give information. Hopefully, it may also be possible to find some schools which are already well into the preparation of G.C.S.E., and display their syllabuses on a sample basis. The Joint 16+ schemes which have operated for some years, and jointly administered by the G.C.E. and C.S.E. boards, can provide sample projects, examination papers and tapes of oral assessments as indicating the nature of the changes alongside the G.C.S.E. papers which will be taken. Such a conference might conceivably take the following form:

1. Short opening address by the chairperson of the education committee, who will previously have been briefed, and who will hopefully introduce the theme in a positive and sympathetic manner.
2. Three short addresses setting out the nature of the changes by
(a) The Chief Education Officer or other senior officers of the authority, dealing with the overall pedagogic notions as well as hte resource implications.
(b) A prominent local teacher dealing with aspects

A PLAN FOR ACTION

of school implementation.
(c) A senior person from the examination group who should stress the co-operative nature of the exercise, the ways in which partnership between examination boards and local authorities can function, with a brief overview of the constitution and functioning of the examining group. Suitable publicity material should of course, have been distributed beforehand. None of these addresses should be too long and speakers be given a time limit. This is often overlooked, with the result that worthwhile enterprises turn into lecture sessions, which are never well received by local politicians, who prefer to talk themselves. Such a first session might well be concluded within an hour, or ninety minutes at the most.

The second session should enable such a conference to be divided into groups, covering the major themes of the examination of change. The following list of themes suggests itself, but is of course, by no means exclusive.

The need for change - an overview.
Implementation of G.C.S.E. at school level.
Training programmes.
Resource implications.
Co-operation between LEA's and examining groups.
The national criteria - aspects of a new relationship.
Communication and publicity - scope for partnership between schools and local authorities.
Further topics for those especially interested to look at one aspect in greater depths, could also be arranged to cover say, the new grading schemes, criteria referencing, aspects of assessment and the approach to key subjects, especially English and mathematics. A session on oral examining is highly desirable. Clearly, such sessions should be led by the professionals, who will themselves need to give careful thought to a compact, but effective presentation.

One of the problems in local government politics has been the shift away from the influence of the professionals, towards the politicians in the decision making process in matters of detail. This is not the place to argue the pros and cons of such a development; suffice it to say that in an exercise as far reaching and complex as the introduction of the new examination system, the expertise does not exist among politicians and

151

A PLAN FOR ACTION

there is a clear responsibility for the professional staff of educators to take the initiative in briefing and explaining. A discussion group chaired by a lay committee member, but addressed, say for ten or fifteen minutes by a professional, is therefore a good way of proceeding. The tendency which one has lately found in some local education authorities to ensure that 'the say' is always with the politicians, with the professionals tendering advice when asked, is not appropriate for an exercise of this kind. The number of practising teachers and personnel of examination boards present should be sufficient in numbers, and of high quality to make an impact. The cross fertilisation of ideas with members can take place in group discussions, and will be substantially enhanced by such a mixture. There is no point in arranging such a conference if education committee members of whatever party, simply talk to themselves, without having the proper opportunity of meeting those particularly concerned with implementing the change. Such a conference can be accommodated in a day, or two half days. Such a time scale does not of course, allow treatment in depths, and if it can be stretched to a couple of days, so much the better. The need will be for some practical workshop sessions, in which members themselves can be involved in a learning process, rather than further lectures and discussions. Half-a-day, though short, is not a waste of time if properly planned and presented. Some local authorities have organised meetings of this kind in connection with aspects of special education or other major issues and these have proved entirely useful. A G.C.S.E. orientated conference could be the first of a number of enterprises which would not need to be frequent, but should be launched at various times during the early years of G.C.S.E.

There is an even greater need for dialogue with employers. Often, individual schools, or groups of schools, will be the best agencies to initiate the dialogue which is required. Fortunately, links between individual schools and many local firms are well established, so that information relating to the new system and opportunities for discussion will arise naturally from the contacts which already exist. However, short conferences between teachers and employers will do a great deal to encourage both knowledge and acceptance of G.C.S.E. It needs to be recognised that, unlike the situation which existed after the introduction of C.S.E., which had to make its way alongside the well established and highly regarded G.C.E. examination, the situation is different with a common system; the employer has no alternative but to accept what is. Indeed, such evidence as can be gleaned, particularly in the regions, suggests a positive approach to the common system by many employers. The duality of G.C.E. and C.S.E. has caused enough problems to appointment and training personnel, and others responsible for recruitment, for them to be totally aware of its disadvantages. Smaller firms and individual employers have been even less inclined to find time to sort out grade equivalents. Employers are often impatient with the complexities, and what they see as the endless controversies, surrounding examination systems. Anything which simplifies the procedures is welcomed by them. It has also been notable that in discussions on the grading system, the employers themselves have said that a five point scheme is sufficient for their purposes, and may well emerge as the teachers' allies in simplifying the seven grades, A, B, C, D, E, F, G into the first five which are commonly acknowledged to discriminate sufficiently between examinees.

Three models for meetings with employers may be considered:
1. <u>The school model</u>. Here, the school itself invites representatives of employers to meet teaching staffs, to explain and discuss the change. Again, supporting materials, exhibitions of the kind mentioned earlier, and a structure whereby the head and/or other teaching staff explain the changes in an opening session, encouraging contributions from employers to emphasise the partnership between school and the world of work, to be followed by discussion groups on relevant themes, is entirely useful. The selection of such themes, should relate closely to matters of immediate concern to the employers; in particular, an explanation of alternative papers, the timing of the new examination, the special position of Easter leavers, the fact that pupils who previously took C.S.E. were available for full-time employment only from the end of May, but under the new system will be able to return to school to take the examination if already in employment, are all vital issues which have not, as yet, been fully publicised. The present scarcity of jobs for school leavers highlights the need for employers to be fully aware of the impact of the change on the output of school leavers, which will be reduced to once a year

A PLAN FOR ACTION

(June/July) and yet allow greater flexibility as schools will be able to enter candidates who have already left. The school model is particularly appropriate where links already exist, where schools and employers know each other, and where a joint enterprise of the kind mentioned will be well received.

Again, the question must arise as to where the time is to come from. Many schools sometimes arrange such employers sessions immediately after the end of the school day, say between 4.0.p.m. - 6.0.p.m., with school perhaps finishing somewhat earlier than is normally the case. It would certainly be more than justified in present circumstances, to shorten an afternoon session to enable such a meeting to take place.

The area model.

A second model is for an employers' conference to be organised on an area basis. Here, groups of schools in conjunction with the local careers and area education office, or the local teachers' centre, could arrange suitable meetings and sessions, preferably during the school day. A decision will need to be taken as to who initiates such an enterprise; the invitation could come from a group of schools acting jointly either through the area education office, the teachers' centre or the careers officer. The local advisory groups which many C.S.E. boards have established, are entirely suitable as a basis for area meetings, as all local schools are represented. However, what is really important is that such meetings should take place as part of launching the new examination system, to inform local employers, to ensure that the dialogue with teachers takes place, and to create the positive climate with G.C.S.E., needs to establish itself. The deficiencies of the new system should not be hidden: the time scale is extremely short as far as the schools are concerned, but are not necessarily conceived so by employers who have been aware of discussions that seem to them to have dragged on for years. The new assessment techniques, the new grading scheme, the impact of national criteria, both in the general and subjects specific sense, are all features which need to be communicated and are likely to be welcomed by employers, many of whom have never been wholly converted to purely school based syllabuses. At the same time, the reformist nature of the changes and particularly the considerable importance attached to the continuous assessment, are features which will be regarded as positive in themselves, since many employers are accustomed to such approaches through their own training and related further education programmes.

The third model is to use the examination boards and groups in a purposeful and sensitive way to acknowledge and further the employers' interests. Employers' representatives already sit on the C.S.E. boards, and often on some of their major committees. It is likely that the constitution of the new examining groups will reflect this co-operation, and the initiation of meetings with the employers by the examination boards will therefore have a spring board by using the usually co-opted employers. Precedents already exist: thus, the East Anglian C.S.E. board arranged a productive meeting in Norwich, and plans are afoot for further meetings in the region. The regional approach to such meetings may well be the most useful using existing C.S.E. board areas. Such a programme will require co-ordination by the whole examining group, but there is no difficulty in working out a strategy covering the region, with perhaps one major function arranged by the examining group as such to which key employers, as well as representative of diverse interests of industry and commerce in the area serviced by the group, should be invited. It will certainly be necessary to ensure that the identity of an examining group is known to employers, whilst at the same time, explaining briefly methods of co-operation in what will be larger groupings.

Whichever method is chosen, the essential point is to bring about a dialogue to inform, to explain and to ensure that the nature and significance of the change is communicated by those most intimately concerned with it, rather than allow a situation to develop where such information is gleaned from articles or news items which often surface at points of controversy. In all these initiatives, the proper and legitimate interests of trade unions should not be overlooked. In launching a new educational reform and identifying target groups and new procedures, the young persons who will enter into commerce, are also the trade unionists of the future. Whenever possible, an opportunity should be taken to invite trade unionists alongside employers, or if thought convenient, alongside other interest groups, to help in the promotion of the new system. The need to provide appropriate literature to the trade unions, to ensure that the unions are represented on the groups in the same way as the

A PLAN FOR ACTION

employers, and are accorded appropriate status and recognition, must be recognised. All this is best done in conjunction with the approach to employers, because for the young school leavers the trade unions are part of the world of work. Programmes should therefore stress the identity of interests which both sides of industry have in launching a good examination system, avoiding undue controversy.

A particular challenge for those responsible for implementing the G.C.S.E., will be in the relationship with the Manpower Services Commission. The educational objectives of the Technical and Vocational Initiative (TVEI) differ from those of the new examination system and their application to the school world, and contain the seeds of potential conflict. The emphasis in TVEI on definite and designated vocational orientation, on assessment procedures which originate outside the educational fraternity, the considerable additional resource provision for a minority of pupils, and the controversial nature of the scheme, are likely to lead to an uneasy co-existence of G.C.S.E. with TVEI, and this will pose special problems for teachers working in both areas. However, there are also some hopeful signs: some TVEI schemes have already been submitted by schools to the examination boards for validation and recognition within the existing G.C.E. and C.S.E. framework, and there is no reason why a potential area of conflict should not be turned into one of co-operation. Whatever the future of TVEI, whatever the ethics of the political decisions whereby very large sums of money are separated from the main stream of educational provisions, and allocated to the few on the basis of judgments made by people removed from the schools, the interests of the young people are best served by moving purposefully towards a progressive integration of TVEI schemes into the G.C.S.E., and so avoiding the emergence of another dual system - the very thing it seeks to replace. Such an approach will be controversial and may well be resisted, particularly by those responsible for delivering the heavy vocational bias in most TVEI schemes. On the other hand, it should be clearly recognised that the young people engaged on TVEI will themselves expect and be expected, to have recognised qualifications at the end of their courses. It is highly doubtful whether an assessment scheme concentrating on the skill element, but leaving out the general educational dimension which G.C.S.E. provides, will prove to be either as durable or as acceptable as conventional examinations, given the nature of educational change. The way forward is therefore for flexibility on the part of both the M.S.C. and examining groups, and the clear recognition that procedures exist whereby TVEI schemes can be both authenticated and certificated as G.C.S.E. subjects, especially under mode 3 procedures. There are hurdles to be overcome. How many TVEI schemes conform to national criteria? Has anyone suggested that they should, or is TVEI exempt from national policy? How can the grading system be used to certify attainment in schemes with a different orientation? How will criteria referencing, when it gets off the ground, be related to TVEI schemes which contain assessment techniques which differ from what is envisaged for G.C.S.E? Here, we can only note that problems exist, but given goodwill on both sides, and the creation of an educational climate which moves towards harmony rather than confrontation, they are soluble. All parties concerned, but especially government, have a clear responsibility to promote actively that harmony.

A plan for action is also required to ensure that the further and higher education interests and in particular, the teaching training establishments, become part of the partnership which the new examination system requires if it is to be successful. With regard to higher education, this is likely to prove an easier task than was the case with the establishment of C.S.E. The G.C.E. boards, with only minor exceptions, are already part of our higher education system through their links with universities. Higher education and university interests are represented alongside those of the schools and the local education authorities in the new examination group structures at all levels: teachers from schools, colleges and universities launching the new subjects for G.C.S.E., have met at subject panel level, representing both school and higher education interests. To some extent, the deficiencies, and occasional rigidities of a few new syllabuses are themselves the result of the need for compromise in accommodating two different philosophies - the need to provide a basis for examining academic excellence for a minority, and also to provide certification for nearly the whole ability range. But the community of interests is greater than any differences, for the higher education fraternity inevitably relies on what the schools provide. The essential tasks which present

A PLAN FOR ACTION

themselves relate to the acceptability of grades for entry to higher education courses and in particular, to develop a thorough understanding and acceptance of syllabuses which include substantial elements of teacher assessed components. On the first issue the need will be for flexibility. Although examination grades obtained at 16 or earlier in the G.C.E. and C.S.E. examinations by sixth formers seeking entrance to the degree courses, do not play the decisive part as do the vital 'A' level grades, it is well known that earlier examination results which appear on UCCA forms and polytechnic applications are significant elements in deciding the nature of offers made to applicants. The paramount need is for higher education selectors to understand, accept and be sympathetic to the new system which will take time to settle down. Any rigidity in evaluating the potential of candidates in terms of the highest grades only, could lead to serious errors of judgment. The need is for liberalism and flexibility.

The same applies when making judgments about syllabuses containing substantial parts of school based assessment. In essence, this is after all no different from what the universities practise themselves. They award their own degrees and employers of graduates in both the public and the private sectors, are expected to accept the validity and accuracy of their judgments. The acceptance of similar judgments made by teachers in schools, reflecting at least part of a candidates' performance, is long overdue here and has for many years been well established in the examination systems of other countries, notably Germany, France and central European countries such as Austria. It is to be hoped therefore, that a warm welcome will be given to the change by higher education interests. The presence of many university people on G.C.E. boards and in particular, the powerful part played by the G.C.E. secretaries and most of their colleagues from the higher education sector who are closely connected with the launching of the system, clearly recognises this and there are already signs that many are very good ambassadors in senior common rooms and at faculty meetings. There also needs to be, on the part of school teachers, a recognition that university statutes, the nature of university government and the ethos of academic life brings with it certain constraints, which cannot be simply ignored or swept away. The very independence of the universities is in itself a positive element in launching the new system. The universities and the G.C.E. boards will need to accommodate the inevitable change of direction in a system geared towards examining the vast majority of the school population rather than a small number. Although the responsibilities of G.C.E. boards are for the higher grades, A, B and C only, and those of the C.S.E. boards for candidates who obtain Grade D or lower, this is entirely artificial. The new examining system is a joint system, and should be administered jointly. The division of responsibility between G.C.E. and C.S.E. boards, as laid down by the Secretary of State, is a political rather than a professional or pedagogic device, and is not likely to survive for too long. The 16+ syllabuses on which many pupils are already being examined have been devised jointly by both sets of boards, and joint decision making procedures on all aspects, including syllabus development, grading schemes, fee structures and appeal machinery are already established. This is the model which should be followed in the future.

In the higher education sector, the time scale for accommodating the changes is more comfortable than in the schools, since the first substantial numbers of 'A' level entrants with G.C.S.E. qualifications will not reach higher education until 1990, allowing sufficient time for the information to percolate and areas of co-operation to become firmly established. Again, the presence of higher education representatives on the new examining groups will be a vital factor in helping this co-operation, and should, wherever possible, be accompanied by reciprocal arrangements. The more practising school teachers and officers of examining groups and boards find their way into the counsels of higher education, whether it be by co-options or election, the better the quality of the dialogue.

The world of further education has always been more closely connected with the schools than that of higher education. Further education colleges will receive substantial numbers of candidates with G.C.S.E. qualifications in 1989, a year earlier than the higher education sector. Entrance requirements to courses will need to be adjusted in G.C.S.E. terms, and provision be made for the taking of the G.C.S.E. examination in colleges of further education and in technical colleges. Unlike C.S.E., G.C.S.E. is not entirely a school based examination, and will find its way into further

A PLAN FOR ACTION

examination establishments as G.C.E. has done for many years. The reciprocal arrangements between examination boards and further education interests, which are a minor feature of the management of the C.S.E. examination, have perhaps not been as widely accepted as both sides would have wished, and will clearly need strengthening. Here, there is room for further co-operation and development, which is already emerging, though not without growing pains in the difficult and controversial areas of various 17+ examinations. However, since there is the requirement that G.C.S.E., like G.C.E., must be made available to mature candidates (the national criteria makes specific mention of the need to accommodate such candidates), the community of interests which exists between the schools, the examining groups and further and higher education establishments is clearly visible and should override sectional interests. The examining groups are charged with the specific responsibilty to provide suitable syllabuses for the potentially vast numbers of adults who will wish to avail themselves of the G.C.S.E. examination. In a world of increasing leisure and fewer jobs, the potential for G.C.S.E. to make a substantial contribution to adult education in the widest sense is immense.

Another challenge will be to ensure that teacher educators and teacher trainers, are involved alongside their colleagues in schools, in launching the new examination system. Newly trained teachers will be expected, on taking up their first appointments, to be aware of, and show reasonable acquaintance with the major aspects of G.C.S.E. The major elements of G.C.S.E., particularly the grading system, assessment procedures, syllabus construction and the functioning of the examination groups, will need to be identified by teacher trainers and integrated into all professional courses leading to a teaching qualification. This will be a definite advance on what has happened so far, where such courses could comfortably assume that since students in teacher training establishments had themselves passed through the examination system, they would be well acquainted with it, an entirely reasonable assumption. This will not be the case with G.C.S.E., for several years. Future teachers will for some time, have passed through the old examination system, but will be expected to operate the new one on arriving in schools. It is therefore incumbent on the training institutions to arrange seminars, conferences, meetings and discussions to ensure that the teacher training component is not left behind in launching an understanding of G.C.S.E. A good way of doing this is to associate the training establishments firmly both with the schools and the examining groups. A useful beginning could be made by ensuring that all co-opted places offered to teacher training institutions by examining boards are taken up, and that more places are made available, particularly at subject panel level, and also in the overall management structure of the examining groups. Such links need strengthening and developing.

Another feature which may well be considered as a way forward is occasional link appointments and short term secondments. Link appointments between schools and teacher training establishments are still few and far between, and yet this is an area where progress is vital. Here and there exciting schemes exist and certainly the University of East Anglia has made a genuine attempt to meet this need; its School of Education has been most successful in launching a scheme whereby practising teachers are involved in assessing future teachers, and where at least one professor of education has spent a sabbatical term as a member of the staff of a local comprehensive school. Yet another example, growing from the co-operation which existed between the Keswick College of Education and Norfolk and Suffolk schools, prior to the establishment of the University School of Education, but further developed by it, is the involvement of local teachers in courses at graduate and post-graduate level, and the considerable part played by the University in local INSET schemes. The University School of Education stands extremely well with local teachers, and its positive and encouraging policies are worthy of study by other similar institutions.

Co-operative schemes geared towards G.C.S.E., can be developed and will act as a refresher and stimulant for both school and university teachers. Some arrangements may well have to be of an ad hoc nature, and be instituted quickly, but there is no doubt that they will be extremely useful.

Another possibility are short term secondments for say, a day a week, a whole week, half-a-term, or a term, whereby school teachers and college lecturers exchange jobs. This is not nearly as difficult as it is sometimes made out to be. If a module relating to G.C.S.E. is included in a teacher training programme, and an experienced secondary

A PLAN FOR ACTION

teacher is asked to teach this over a concentrated period, say a week or a fortnight, the college tutor taking his or her timetable at school, much can be achieved with mutual benefit to both sides. The isolationism of which the world of higher education is sometimes accused, and which is often exaggerated, can, nevertheless, exist. G.C.S.E. provides an excellent opportunity to develop a partnership between school and college, which both sides want and need.

The tasks which have been identified in publicising G.C.S.E., beyond the walls of the classroom demand time, skill and faith in the success of the new system without abandoning the constructive criticism needed to improve it. Much of what has been suggested can be done, in stages or phases, by the teachers in schools, providing they feel that they have the necessary support from parents, local education authorities, employers, the work of higher and further education and the general public at large. Such support is not easily come by, and a climate needs to be created where it is forthcoming. The teaching profession has shown, over the years, that it usually rises to a challenge: the launching of the reforms of the 1944 Education Act, the creation of comprehensive schools, the detailed work of complex and complicated examination systems all depended to a large extent for their success on the teachers in the schools. It is a lesson always to be remembered, particularly by those in high places, with political power and the ability to command the purse strings. The teachers, given the tools, will do the job.

Chapter Seven

REFERENCES

(1) <u>G.C.S.E. - The new exam system at 16 plus - a leaflet for parents.</u> DES publication 1985.
(2) Professor G. Brown spent a term teaching at the Hewett School in the summer of 1985.

APPENDIX

GCSE EXAMINING GROUPS IN ENGLAND AND WALES

Groups & constituent boards		Address for enquiries
	London & East Anglia Group	
GCE:	University of London School Examinations Board	London University Stewart House 32 Russell Sq. LONDON WC1B 5DN
CSE:	East Anglian Examinations Board	"The Lindens" Lexden Road COLCHESTER CO3 3RL
	London Regional Examining Board	Lyon House 104 Wandsworth High Street LONDON SW18 4LF
	Southern Group	
GCE:	University of Oxford Delegacy of Local Examinations	Ewert Place Summertown OXFORD OX2 7BZ
	Associated Examining Board	Wellington House Station Road ALDERSHOT Hants. GU11 1BQ
CSE:	Southern Regional Examinations Board	53 London Road SOUTHAMPTON SO9 4YL

	South East Regional Examinations Board	Beloe House 2 and 4 Mount Ephraim Road TUNBRIDGE WELLS TN1 1EU
	South Western Examinations Board	23-29 Marsh St. BRISTOL BS1 4BP
	Northern Group	
GCE:	Joint Matriculation Board	MANCHESTER M15 6EU
CSE:	Associated Lancashire Schools Examining Board	12 Harter St. MANCHESTER M60 7LH
	North Regional Examinations Board	Wheatfield Road Westerhope NEWCASTLE-UPON TYNE NE5 5JZ
	North West Regional Examinations Board	Orbit House Albert Street Eccles MANCHESTER M30 0WL
	The Yorkshire and Humberside Regional Examinations Board	31-33 Springfield Avenue, HARROGATE HG1 2HW
	Midland Group	
GCE:	University of Cambridge Local Examinations Syndicate	Syndicate Buildings, 1 Hills Road, CAMBRIDGE CB1 2EU
	Oxford and Cambridge Schools Examinations Board	Elsfield Way OXFORD OX2 8EP and Brook House 10 Trumpington Street CAMBRIDGE CB2 1QB

	Southern Universities' Joint Board for Schools Examinations	Cotham Road BRISTOL BS6 6DD
C.S.E:	East Midlands Regional Examinations Board	Robins Wood House, Robins Wood Road ASPLEY Nottingham NG8 3NH
	The West Midlands Examinations Board	Norfolk House Smallbrook Queensway BIRMINGHAM 5 4NJ

Wales

GCE and CSE	Welsh Joint Education Committee	245 Western Ave. CARDIFF CF5 2YX

INDEX

Anglian Water Authority 31
Art & Design 24, 25, 37, 38, 49
Assistant Masters & Mistresses Association (AMMA) 94
Associated Examining Board 2, 19, 80, 81, 104 105, 163
Associated Lancashire Schools Exam Board. 80, 81, 164
Astronomy 31

Beloe Committee 4, 5, 6, 11, 17, 19
Biology 7, 24, 25, 29, 30
Brown G. Professor 163
Business Studies 24, 25, 36, 49
Cambridge University Examinations Syndicate 2, 9, 50, 80, 81, 164
Careers Officers 137
Carlisle Mark 10
Chamber of Commerce Certificate 3
Chemistry 7, 24, 25, 30
City & Guilds Certificate 3
Classical Studies 24, 25, 35, 40, 49
Cockcroft Report 27, 59
Cockcroft Sir Wilfred 10, 96
Computer Studies 24, 25, 38, 39, 49
Confederation of British Industry (CBI) 94
Craft, Design & Technology (CDT). 24, 25, 38, 49, 51, 53, 64
Criteria - General 22, 29, 40, 46, 47, 60, 64
Criteria - Grade Related 44, 51
Criteria - Norm Referencing 11, 50, 51, 55, 59
Criteria - Referencing 11, 51, 55, 59 60, 64, 72
Criteria - Subject specific 22, 24, 25, 26, 30, 34, 40, 60

Department of Education & Science 21, 24, 25, 29, 39, 40, 45, 61, 67, 78, 96, 98-9, 138, 141, 149
Distinction Certificate 12, 49

East Anglian Exam Board 5, 9, 34, 80, 81, 89, 155, 163
East Midlands Exam

167

INDEX

Board 80, 81, 165
Economics 24, 25, 35, 36, 49
Education Act 1944 1, 2, 162
Eleven Plus 2, 3, 7
English 4, 6, 7, 24, 25, 26, 28, 42, 49, 145, 151
English Literature 26, 27, 49

French 24, 25, 33

Geography 7, 24, 25, 49
Graded Tests 60, 62
Grading Scheme 12, 48, 72, 142, 144, 161

Handicapped candidates 90-91
Her Majesty's Inspectors (Inspectorate) 25, 97, 138
Hewett School 133
History 4, 7, 24, 25, 34-37, 40, 49, 51-52, 67
Home Economics 24, 25, 30-32, 49
Home Economics - Child Development 31
Home Economics - Dress 31, 32
Home Economics - Textile 31, 32

Institute of Home Economics 31

Joint Council for GCE/CSE 99, 100, 105
Joint Council for National Criteria 11, 98, 99
Joint Matriculation Board (JMB) 2, 80, 81, 94-95, 164
Joseph - Sir Keith 4, 10, 13, 21, 29, 78, 96, 135, 145

London & East Anglian Exam Group 13, 34, 81, 88, 92, 163
London Regional Exam Board 80, 81, 89, 163
London University Examinations Board 2, 80, 81, 89, 104, 163

Manpower Services Commission (M.Sc) 156, 157
Mathematics 4, 6, 24-28, 42, 49, 53, 55, 56, 59, 60, 64, 151
Mathematics - Additional 149
Merit Certificate 12, 49
Midland Exam Group 13, 81, 164
Mode 1 5, 20, 39, 82
Mode 2 5, 20, 26, 72, 82, 97, 146
Mode 3 5, 20, 23, 26, 29, 39, 43, 45, 72, 83, 97, 146
Modern Languages 4, 33
Music 24, 25, 38, 49, 60, 89

National Association of Headteachers (NAHT) 94
National Association of Teachers in Higher Education (NATFHE) 94
National Association of Schoolmasters & Union of Women Teachers NAS/UWT 13, 94
National Union of Teachers (NUT) 13, 94, 96, 103, 104

INDEX

Needlework 31
Newsom Report 6, 17
Norfolk 161
Northern Exam Group 13, 81, 94, 101, 104, 164
Northern Ireland Exam Board 18, 81, 97
Northern Regional Exam Board 80, 81, 164
North-West Regional Exam Board 80, 81, 164
Nuttall, Desmond 17

Open University 2, 70, 78
Orr, Lee 17
Oxford & Cambridge Board 80, 81, 164
Oxford Delegacy 80, 81, 163

Physics 7, 24, 25, 29, 50, 60
Popham, W. S. 60, 64
Profiles 15, 60, 61, 138

Records of Achievements 15, 60, 61
Religious Studies 24, 25, 33, 34, 40, 49

School Certificate 1, 15, 134
Schools Council 9, 10, 17, 35, 96, 99
Science 24, 25, 28, 30, 49
Science - Agricultural 30
Science - Applied 30
Science - Engineering 30
Science - Environmental 30
Science - General 30
Science - Rural 30
Science - Social 24, 37
Secondary Examinations Council 10, 21, 24, 26, 29, 39, 44, 61, 70, 78, 84, 96-97, 105, 136, 141, 146
Secondary Heads Association (SHA) 94
Social Studies 49
South-East Regional Exam Board 80, 81, 164
Southern Exam Group 13, 81, 85-88, 96, 104, 163
Southern Regional Exam Board 81, 163
Southern Universities Joint Board 80, 81, 165
South-West Regional Exam Board 81, 164
Standing Conference of CSE Boards 20, 100
Suffolk

Technical & Vocational Educational Initiative (TVEI) 15, 62, 93, 156-7
Technology 28
Trade Union Council 94

UCCA forms 138, 154
Union of Educational Institutes 3
University of East Anglia 161
University of East Anglia - School of Education 161

Waddell - Committe 9, 17
Wales 63, 80, 81, 165
Welsh 24, 33, 49
Welsh Exam Group 13, 165
Welsh Joint Committee 80, 81, 104, 165
West Midlands Exam Board 80, 81, 165
West Yorkshire & Lindsey Exam Board 5, 80, 81
Weston, Peter 105
Williams, Shirley 9

Yorkshire & Humberside Regional Exam Board 81, 164
Youth Training Scheme

169